AWAKENED

AWAKENED

A Divine Healing From Drug Addiction

By Erin Kalte

With Lisa Kalte

Developmental Editor - Cynthia Cutts

authorHOUSE®

AuthorHouse™
1663 Liberty Drive
Bloomington, IN 47403
www.authorhouse.com
Phone: 1-800-839-8640

First published by AuthorHouse 3/22/2011

ISBN: 978-1-4567-4008-5 (e)
ISBN: 978-1-4567-4009-2 (dj)
ISBN: 978-1-4567-4010-8 (sc)

Library of Congress Control Number: 2011901895

Printed in the United States of America

Any people depicted in stock imagery provided by Thinkstock are models,
and such images are being used for illustrative purposes only.
Certain stock imagery © Thinkstock.

This book is printed on acid-free paper.

Because of the dynamic nature of the Internet, any web addresses or links contained in
this book may have changed since publication and may no longer be valid. The views
expressed in this work are solely those of the author and do not necessarily reflect the
views of the publisher, and the publisher hereby disclaims any responsibility for them.

Scripture taken from the HOLY BIBLE, NEW INTERNATIONAL VERSION®. Copyright
© 1973, 1978, 1984 Biblica. Used by permission of Zondervan. All rights reserved.

The "NIV" and "New International Version" trademarks are registered
in the United States Patent and Trademark Office by Biblica. Use
of either trademark requires the permission of Biblica.

While "Awakened" is a true story of Erin Kalte's life, many names in the
following pages have been changed to protect the privacy of others.

I would like to dedicate this book to my family

Mom,

You are the most amazing person I know. With out you, I would not be where I am today. You have walked through this journey with me step-by-step. I am forever grateful for the role you have played, and continue to play, in my life.

Erica,

Our lives have had numerous ups and downs all the while sticking by each other's side the entire way. You are my best friend, my other half. I couldn't ask for a better sister.

Dad,

You are the one man in this world where it was truly love at first sight. You are my "Mr. Fix It" my go to guy. I love you unconditionally and will always cherish our relationship.

Michael Robert Kalte
December 5, 1954 – May 19, 2010

CONTENTS

FOREWORD

By Jeff Redmond
Director Celebrate Recovery, Bayside Church, Granite Bay, California

As I sit in the home of my friends Gary and Mary Lou Sanders in Medellin, Colombia, I've been contemplating the great honor of writing this foreword to the book you now hold in your hands. When Erin's mother, Lisa brought Erin to meet with me at Bayside Church in 2008, I knew that God was going to change this young lady's life forever. I recognized the desperation and hopelessness in her eyes.

You see, 16 years prior to my first visit with Erin, I was in the same place. Although I was much older than Erin and my addiction was alcohol instead of drugs, I too had lost everything. I understood the tragedy of losing my family. I had experienced the same hopelessness and desperation and just like Erin, I was in search of a miracle. I finally went to the only place I hadn't tried - the foot of the cross, where I surrendered everything to Jesus. That decision to put my life into the care of the only "True Higher Power," launched me onto a successful road of recovery in every area of my life.

Although in many ways our stories are different, Erin and I both had to come to that place in our life where we could find the courage to step out of denial, share our struggles with someone, and then put our lives in the hands of the only one who could heal and change our lives forever.

As I sat with Erin and Lisa that afternoon, God's holy presence was evident in many ways. The most obvious was when I held Erin's tear stained face in my hands and shared God's unconditional love for her and the promise of a new life. It was a sacred moment, as I realized that the Holy

Spirit was using me as a vessel to share those promises with her. Talk about being humbled! Before we finished our conversation, I was able to suggest that Erin attend the Bayside Church college age group, "The Shore," where she could find some healthy friendships and accountability.

In December of 2008, while sitting in the audience at our pastors' annual "Vision Dessert" for the upcoming year, I was suddenly delighted and blessed as the auditorium went dark and on the big screen "Erin's Story" came to life in front of 2,000 people. I couldn't have been more proud of Erin than I was in that moment. I also knew without any doubt, that her heavenly father was very pleased with his daughter as well. The courage it took for Erin to be honest and transparent as she shared her past, reminded everyone in the auditorium how our God can take the ashes of our lives and turn them into gold for his great purpose.

My prayer for you as you read through the following pages is that you will discover something about yourself that needs God's help to heal and that you will receive, with an open mind and heart, the leading of the Holy Spirit and his truth, as Erin's story begins to unfold. I also pray that you will understand that no matter what your struggle, you can find the courage, with God's help, to step out of denial and surrender your life to the son of the most high, Jesus Christ!

Thank you Erin, for allowing me to be part of your story, and for the humbling opportunity to witness God's gift of healing in your life.

Love ya kiddo!

He said to me, "My grace is sufficient for you, for my power is made perfect in weakness." Therefore I will boast all the more gladly about my weaknesses, so that Christ's power may rest on me. That is why, for Christ's sake, I delight in weaknesses, in insults, in hardships, in persecutions, in difficulties. For when I am weak, then I am strong. 2 Corinthians 12:9-10

In his grace,
Jeff Redmond

INTRODUCTION

My life has *not* been a piece of cake. I feel that I've experienced more in 24 years than most people do in a lifetime. "Awakened" is my journey from a California upper middle class princess, to an out of control rebellious teenager, to a desperate meth addict, fearless of the consequences of the dark drug world. "Awakened" is more than a dramatic tale, it is the story of a divine healing from drug addict to the person God planned for me to be.

The cover of my book is symbolic of the re-creation of me. The cupcake is that All-American girl - the person of substance with a solid foundation.

The cupcake wrapper is my family and friends who wrapped me in their love through all the conflicts and drama of my journey.

The frosting on the cupcake represents my personality - the crazy, goofy, loud girl, who loves to laugh and gives God the glory for every new day. I am often accused of being "over the top" in my enthusiasm and energy, just the same as the frosting.

The sprinkles on the cupcake are a reminder of how my life was shattered by drugs. At the lowest point of my drug addiction I felt as if my life had been shattered into a million pieces with no hope of ever putting it back together.

The candle represents the divine miracle I experienced in being healed from drug addiction. That inner glow that I experience each day I awaken unchained to drug addiction is one of the many miracles God has given me throughout this journey.

At the very top of the cupcake is the sparkler, which symbolizes God, the light of my world, who lights up my life every day. But God isn't just a flickering light from a small birthday candle in my world. God sparks my life with wild, vibrant, noisy fireworks that explode into all areas of my life.

This is my story; a story of a lost soul, re-created to fulfill God's plan. My hope is that as you read "Awakened" you will discover that God has a plan for everyone, and that he can heal you or someone you love, just the same as he has healed me.

In his love,
Erin Kalte

CHAPTER 1

LIVING THE GOOD LIFE

I was a 20-year-old meth addict, living the good life. Unlike all those meth losers, I was living the dream, and life was good. I had a great job, cool car and I lived in a constant state of euphoria. I was surrounded by loyal friends - all drug users - who became my family. There was nothing wrong with my life as a meth addict. I had plenty of money and I was happy - gloriously happy.

After completing cosmetology school in Northern California, I convinced my dad to give me $3000 to move to Los Angeles. My goal was to become a runway stylist in Hollywood and I had a lead on a fabulous job. My friend James invited me to stay with him while I got settled, and soon I was working at the Wilshire Grande Hotel in downtown Los Angeles as a stylist, where I did photo shoots and runway styles for some very prestigious clients.

It was an amazing life. I was 20 years old and working my dream job in the most glamorous city in the world. James and all my new friends in Los Angeles were all into the drug culture and smoking meth was a common practice at our place. It was a perfect world; go to work, make a ton of money in salary and tips, dress in the most fashionable clothes, take in the

Hollywood night life, smoke a lot of meth and party like a rock star. I got my own place and began a serious relationship with a guy named Jackson.

Jackson had an intriguing edge about him. He was tall, with big dark eyes and curly black hair. Jackson not only did drugs, but also sold drugs and soon drugs were the focal point of our relationship. Jackson did all kinds of sketchy things like stealing, selling stolen goods and anything to make money. It didn't bother me; I had abandoned my values a long time ago as I became more involved with meth. Everyone stole – it was just an easy way to get money to pay for more drugs.

The first time Jackson beat me up was on December 15th - the day after his birthday. He went out partying for his birthday without me. It was fine, whatever; I didn't care if he went out with his friends. I had other friends in LA, so while Jackson was out celebrating, I hung out with Trent, a good friend who was like a brother to me. Jackson thought Trent and I had a romantic thing going, but Trent and I were just buddies - smoking buddies - who liked to mellow out together. Beyond that there was nothing for Jackson to be jealous over.

When Jackson and his friend Brad got back from their celebration, they found me with Trent, and Jackson went into a jealous rage. He broke into my place and filled the pickup bed of Brad's truck with everything I owned that he could carry. Then Brad and Jackson drove to Trent's house, where Jackson started throwing my stuff all over the street, the driveway, the lawn - just everywhere.

"What are you doing?" I screamed at him. I've always been a person who stood up for herself and I never took abuse from anyone. I recognized my clothes, my furniture, my CDs, all scattered around my car. I was standing at my car trying to figure out what to do and what Jackson hoped to gain from this tirade.

"Stop!" I demanded, "Stop throwing my stuff around!"

Jackson hopped down from the pickup bed and stormed over to me. Before I knew what was happening, he slapped me across the face – hard.

I was stunned. It took me a second to figure out that my boyfriend was physically assaulting me. I'd seen him angry before, but never like this, and never at me. Jackson started yelling and cussing at me, calling me filthy names and accusing me of cheating on him with Trent.

"Why aren't you at your house?" he screamed. "What are you doing here?"

I covered my cheek, trembling, "We're just hanging out," I said. "Trent and I are just friends. You know that."

"You're lying!" he screamed in my face. His dark eyes were wide and he looked like a madman.

"Jackson, I'm just friends with Trent," I said to him calmly. "I didn't lie to you. What's the problem?"

Jackson was in a drunken rage, coupled with whatever drugs he'd taken that night. His violence scared me and looking back I still don't know why I took his abuse. It was not my nature to back down from a confrontation, but I tried to reason with him, with terror pulsating in my ears.

"This is ridiculous," I said to Jackson in what I hoped was a voice of reason. "It's so disrespectful, throwing my stuff everywhere. What are you trying to prove?"

I was still standing beside my car with one arm on the car and the other on the open door. From Jackson's demeanor, I could tell that he wanted to get in my car.

"Move!" Jackson demanded. "Get out of the way."

I recovered some of my emotional strength. "No!" I yelled back. "You're not getting in my car."

It was like I poured gasoline on the raging fire within Jackson. "If you don't move I'm going to beat the crap out of you!" Then he slapped me hard three more times across my face.

I'm a small-built woman, about 5' 3" and at the time of this incident, I weighed maybe 90 pounds. Jackson was a big guy, over 200 pounds and built like an NFL player. He easily doubled me in size.

With little effort, Jackson picked me up off the ground and literally threw me across the street. I hit the pavement hard and rolled several times before I hit the curb. I was dressed in expensive dress slacks and a silk shirt and I remember thinking that both were surely ruined from the blood staining them.

I didn't move. I just stayed crumpled in the street, afraid to move, certain that I had sustained serious injury. Trent and his friend had been sitting on a bench in front of his house and saw what happened.

Trent jumped up, "Whoa Bro," Trent said to Jackson. "This isn't cool. You can't do this in front of my house."

I could hear Trent's words, as I trembled there in the street, scraped up and in pain. Slowly I pulled myself up and decided to just get away. I headed back to my car and all the while Jackson was yelling at me, calling me "stupid" and a whole string of filthy names.

When I tried to get in my car, Jackson shoved me into the back seat as he got in the driver's seat. Brad got in the passenger side and together they kidnapped me.

After robbing me of all my money and credit cards, they made a run through a fast food drive-up window and then Jackson took Brad back to pick up his truck, which was still parked at Trent's house. I thought they were both going to get in Brad's truck and let me go – I thought this nightmare was over, but I discovered that it had just begun. After dropping Brad off, Jackson took off with my car, driving me up into the hills of Pasadena. Brad followed in his pickup.

Houses are spread far apart in the neighborhood where we were and I realized that we were getting into a more rural and remote area the farther we drove. After driving around for nearly an hour, Jackson parked my car. From the back seat I watched as he took my purse and both sets of keys. I was terrified. Jackson was still so angry and in his drugged and alcohol haze he was unreasonable.

He looked over the seat at me, narrowing his eyes. "I'm leaving you here," he glared at me. "If I come back here tomorrow and you're not in this car, I'll track you down and kill you." He looked directly into my eyes with a cold stare. Then he got out of my car, slammed the car door and climbed into the cab of Brad's truck, which was idling next to my car. The two of them drove away.

Los Angeles is known for its balmy winter weather, but that December night, up in the hills above Pasadena, it was very cold. I didn't have a coat or a jacket and there wasn't a blanket in my car. I was so cold. My body hurt from hitting the pavement and I was still bleeding. I knew I needed medical attention, but I was paralyzed with fear, wondering if Jackson was out there watching me or if he really would come back and kill me. I was crying and I couldn't sleep. I found a sweatshirt on the floor in the backseat and wrapped it around my legs, trying to stay warm. I kept shaking with panic and cold. In exhaustion and fear I finally sobbed myself asleep in the cold car. I woke up to sunlight warming my bruised face.

Slowly I raised my head, peaking out over the front seat to see if Jackson was out there. I noticed a woman up the road with two dogs. I got out of my car, and limped up to her, confused and terrified. She could see that I'd been beaten and my tears wouldn't stop.

"Are you okay?" this kind stranger asked, "You need medical care. What happened?"

"Can I use your phone?" I asked, choking back my sobs and hiccups.

"Of course you can use the phone, honey," she said. "But I think I should get you some help. Do you need an ambulance or a police officer?"

"No," I told her. "Thank you so much. I just need to use your phone."

This woman was so sweet. She put the dogs inside her SUV and then ran inside, and came out with a bottle of water and a blanket. I sat down on a patio chair and hugged the blanket around my shivering shoulders. "Thank you," I told her as I began to warm up. She ran back inside and brought a cordless phone outside.

"I'm so sorry, but I really need to be somewhere," she explained, gesturing to the car and her dogs. "Are you sure you don't want some medical attention? Or maybe to call the police?"

"No," I said. "I'll be okay. I just need to make a phone call and I'll be on my way."

"Okay, honey," the woman said. "Use what you need here and just leave the phone on the patio table when you're done." She climbed into her car with the dogs and backed out of her driveway, leaving me alone with the phone.

As I watched her drive away, I picked up the phone, and then it hit me - I didn't have anyone to call. I gasped as I realized that I'd lost all the people I could count on to help me in an emergency. My mom and dad were both tired of my lies and deceit; my sister couldn't help me, and I surely wasn't going to call Jackson. I took a deep breath and I called Trent.

Trent picked up on the second ring. "Trent, I don't know what to do," I said. "Jackson and Brad kidnapped me and then left me without my ID, money, phone or car keys. I've been freezing up here and I don't even know where I am." I started crying all over again.

Trent was so glad to hear my voice. "Erin! I didn't know what they were going to do with you!" Trent exclaimed. "Where are you?"

I sighed and tried to calm down. "I don't know where I am. I think I'm somewhere in the hills above Pasadena, but I don't recognize anything."

"Well, walk down a block or two and find some cross streets," Trent said. "If you can figure out where you are, I'll come and get you."

So I walked up and down these long, winding streets in the hills above Pasadena, trying to find cross streets. I'd find a street name, and go back to call Trent, but it took several tries before he figured out how to find me.

After about an hour, Trent and another friend came to get me. But once they got there, I honestly didn't know if I should leave. Jackson's threat to kill me if I wasn't there when he returned echoed in my head.

"Let's go," Trent encouraged me. But I was nervous. This all started because Jackson thought I was cheating on him with Trent. Now Trent was the one to rescue me. If Jackson found out Trent was helping me, there was no telling what might happen.

After thinking about it for a minute or two, I finally agreed. "Okay. But I don't want anyone to see me with you." So I left my car there in the hills and hid in the back seat of Trent's car, afraid that Jackson would see me.

Lying in that back seat, just a few hours before being kidnapped in a similar situation, was the first time I recall thinking that perhaps this drug culture lifestyle wasn't as easy or wonderful as I'd been thinking it was. I kept thinking that this couldn't be happening and that it must be some kind of weird nightmare that would pass.

Vividly I remember that I truly didn't know what to do. I was scared beyond belief and even with Trent's friendship, I felt so alone. When we got to Trent's house, I went inside and asked if I could take a shower. While I was in the shower, Jackson called.

"Trent, I need your help," Jackson told him. "I need you to take me up to get Erin's car."

Trent played it cool. "Okay," he agreed. "But I can't do it right now. I'll have to wait to borrow my Grandma's car. Can you give me a half hour?"

As soon as I got out of the shower, Trent took me back to my car; and then he went to get Jackson. While Trent was en route to Jackson's house, I used the kind woman's phone again. This time I called Jackson.

"I need my keys and my stuff," I told him with resolve. "Just give me my purse, my phone and my keys and I won't call the cops."

I thought he must have sobered up, because he agreed. "Just come and get them, and you can have them," he told me.

So I walked back down those hills to retrieve my phone, keys and purse from Jackson. It took me over an hour to get there. I was so sore from being thrown onto the pavement from the night before, but I kept walking until finally I got there.

Jackson came outside to greet me. But instead of giving me the stuff I came to pick up, he told me that he'd changed his mind and he wasn't going to give me my car keys or my purse or my money.

"But Jackson!" I was mad. I pushed aside my fear and lashed out in anger. I screamed at him. "I just walked over an hour to get here! Don't play with me. I'm exhausted, I'm hurt, just give me my stuff."

Jackson loved tormenting me. "No, you can go back to your car and I'll come and get you when I'm ready." He turned on his heel and went back into the house and left me standing there.

With nowhere else to go, I began the hour long walk back up those winding hills to my car. I returned to the house where I could use the phone and called Jackson again. "I'm going to call the police and press charges," I warned him. "If you don't bring me my keys and my purse, I'm going to call the cops."

The threat of the police got his attention and Jackson agreed to return my personal things. So I walked back down the long hills again to get the things he had taken. This time Jackson gave me my things, but he kept one set of my keys for himself. There was an evil tension between us and I was afraid to go back to my apartment. So I walked back to my car and went to San Fernando, back to my friend James.

James took one look at me and became furious. "Erin, you have to get out of that relationship. Jackson is bad for you."

I listened to James rant on about Jackson and I knew that he was right, but I didn't know what to do or where else to go. Before I could even point that out, James insisted that I stay with him.

"This is crazy, Erin." James was adamant. "You need to stay away from him. Stay here. Stay with me."

I breathed a sigh of relief. "Okay," I agreed.

I spent the next couple of weeks hanging out at James' house. I kept thinking, "Wow. So this is my life. My life is crazy now." I went back to work part time, coming straight back to James' house, lying low and resting. I decided that I'd try to get off drugs, to put the meth out of my life and rebuild my career. Even with that resolve, I kept doing drugs with James as I recovered from my wounds.

After a couple of weeks, I went back to work full-time. One day after work, I decided to go back to Jackson's house and get my extra set of keys. I was dressed up, my hair was styled and I looked like my usual fashionable self. Even a meth addict wants to look good.

I knocked on Jackson's door, and when he answered, he smiled broadly and acted like nothing had gone wrong between us.

"Wow! Erin, you look beautiful!" Jackson hugged me. "Where the heck have you been? I've really missed you!"

Gently I pushed back his hug, and smiled. "Thanks, Jackson, but I'm just here for my keys. You still have my extra keys and I really need them."

"Oh, sure," Jackson agreed. He pushed the door wide open. "No problem. Come on inside. Why don't you stay for awhile and smoke with us."

And just like that, I agreed. I went inside, forgetting and forgiving the brutality of my last encounter with this man and the string of felonies he had committed against me. Soon I was back hanging out with Jackson, smoking meth with him daily, getting involved in his sketchy lifestyle and enjoying the edginess of the drug world.

Jackson and I settled into a routine of smoking meth, selling drugs and hanging out. I always drove us anywhere we went, since Jackson didn't have a car or a driver's license. Even in Los Angeles, this wasn't a problem for Jackson, because since he always had drugs, people drove him wherever he wanted to go. I moved back into my apartment, and Jackson lived in a big house with his family. Drugs were our world.

One night we had smoked a little meth, then went out for awhile. I dropped him off at his house and started back to my place. On the way, I stopped to get gas. I had been up from a meth high for about four or five days and I looked horrible. I was dressed okay, in jeans and a sweatshirt, but I had huge bags under my eyes and my complexion was gray.

As I pumped the gas, I noticed a police car in the gas station parking area, with two cops in it. I was terrified of cops, because I knew I was in violation of many laws with my drug use and if I got pulled over, I'd be in big trouble. I finished filling my gas tank, turned the gas cap tight and got into the car. As I left the station, I saw the squad car pull out behind me into traffic. Within seconds, red and blue lights were flashing behind me.

"Oh no!" I thought. I'd smoked meth a few hours ago, and I hoped that my eyes weren't too dilated. I was even more panicked because I had forged vehicle registration and insurance documents in my car. This was not good.

I don't remember what the cops said to me, but before I knew it they were searching my car and going through my purse. I held my breath - I knew that inside my makeup bag there was a foil with a tiny bit of meth in it.

The cops placed me under arrest for possession of drugs, put me in handcuffs and took me to jail. I endured the whole booking process – finger prints, mug shot and strip search. Finally they locked me in a single cell; a solid walled room with only a tiny round window in the door. I was coming down from meth, and felt so bad. By the time they were finished with all the processing and paperwork it was close to 4 a.m.

The cell was all concrete, dirty and disgusting. There was a toilet, but no sink, a bench and a blanket. I pulled my hood up over my head and over my cheek to lie down without anything from the jail touching my skin and went to sleep. I woke up the next morning all alone.

The cell was basically sound-proof, and when no one came to check on me, I started pounding on the door. I was experiencing meth withdrawal and hurting, but I focused on my right to make a phone call. I kept pounding on the door, kicking it and screaming that I wanted to make a phone call. No one came, so I kept on pounding and kicking trying to get someone to respond.

"I want my phone call!" I shouted over and over.

Finally someone called from the other side of the door, "You'll get it when we give it to you, now quiet down."

At last, someone was out there! "I want it now!" I demanded. "I know my rights!"

"We'll give you your phone call when you calm down," was the reply.

I kept pounding on the door until finally they gave me my phone call. I walked to the phone area and as I picked up the phone, I was struck by how I didn't really know who to call.

First, I called Mom, but she didn't answer. I called Jackson, but he didn't answer. Next I tried Trent, and he wasn't home either.

"Great," I sulked as they put me back in my cell.

I sat there in that cell most of the day, until a detective came to ask me some questions. I didn't know any answers to the questions, and finally they released me because there wasn't enough evidence to take to the district attorney.

The police released me from jail, but that didn't solve my problem. I didn't know where I was. I'd never been in the city where the jail was. When I was arrested it was late in the evening and I was dressed for the cool night air. When I walked out of the jail it was hot and I was wearing a sweatshirt. I didn't know how I could get home. When they arrested me, they had locked my purse in my car and towed the car. I had no money, no cell phone – nothing! I was walking around asking people at the jail, "How do I get to Pasadena?"

"Take the bus," was the answer. I didn't have money for a bus, so I thought I would just walk.

"How far is Pasadena?" I asked.

"About 20 miles," was the reply.

I was still suffering from meth withdrawal, angry for the circumstances and disoriented. I walked toward the bus stop and asked people which bus I should take and if they could help me pay for it.

Finally an older guy asked me if I needed a ride.

Without even thinking, I said, "Yes I do! I need a ride!" And despite all the warnings my mom and dad had told me growing up, I got into a car with a complete stranger to take me in the direction I hoped was Pasadena.

I sat in the stranger's car, to have this man start asking me, "What are you doing way out here?"

I didn't want to admit to the truth so I made up a story about how my car had broken down and I just needed a ride back to my home. In my head I kept silently pleading, "Please don't rape me, please don't murder me; just drop me off and don't try anything."

We stopped for gas and he bought me a soda. I was so scared, but before long, the stranger dropped me off just around the corner from Jackson's house; and I headed right back to the people, drugs and lifestyle that had gotten me into this mess in the first place.

Living on the fringes of the law was distracting enough that before I knew it, I just stopped going to work and lost my job. Then I found myself involved in a raid by the police and taken into custody again.

Jackson and I were coming back to his house in my car and on this day, Jackson was driving. He had an opened beer can in the cup holder of my car and a huge supply of meth in his jacket, when we saw the flashing red and blue lights of a squad car behind us.

Jackson eased my car to the curb and looked at me. "We are so screwed," he said. "Look what I have." He reached into his jacket and pulled out a plastic bag filled with meth. Without hesitation I grabbed the bag from his hand, and stuffed the meth down in my pants.

I knew something was definitely wrong when the cops walked to the car and one of them said, "Can you step out of the car, please?" He didn't ask to see any identification, registration or insurance card, just, "Step out of the car." I was really alarmed when a second cop car pulled up with flashing lights and screaming siren.

Jackson and I got out of the car and I watched as the cops began to search Jackson. I was told to sit off to the side of the road on a retaining wall that had a ledge on it. So I walked over there and sat down, fearful of what was going to happen. A third police car showed up with a female officer who searched me. She looked in my bra and patted me down, but she didn't find the meth in my pants. She instructed me to sit back down on the ledge.

The cops took turns talking to me and then Jackson, insisting that we were drug dealers. They kept taunting me that Jackson was telling them that all the drug business was mine. They were trying to get me to 'roll over' on Jackson, and turn him in. I kept answering all their questions, with the same comment, "I don't know what you are talking about."

The police officers kept asking questions, and finally told me they were going to search my car.

I sat there on that ledge watching them search. They went through everything. I had several shopping bags in my car filled with personal items. As the police searched, they took everything out of the bags, examined it all and then threw it all over the ground behind the car. It was humiliating to see my clothes, makeup, even my panties lying in the street. The cops took the seats of my car apart, pulled up the carpet and removed the side panels from the doors, searching for evidence of drugs.

About that time a fourth squad car pulled up and this one had a police dog in it. Terrified, I sat on that ledge, knowing that I was going to prison if that dog got near me. By that time, Jackson had been handcuffed and put into the back of a squad car, and all the police officers were focused on my car. I had to get rid of that meth before they finished their search and brought the dog near me! I didn't know what to do; the bag was far too big to swallow the way I knew other addicts hid their drugs.

I was wearing a bulky sweatshirt, and I leaned on my left arm, with my hand behind my back. I noticed the dirt was soft and I began to slowly dig into the soil, creating a hole big enough to bury the meth. I was positioned so it looked like I was just leaning on my arm, and by moving very slowly, no one noticed the movement of my hand beneath my sweatshirt. Keeping my hand hidden in the folds of my sweatshirt, I reached into the back of my pants and pulled out the meth. Then with my hand still hidden behind my back and under my shirt, I dropped the bag of drugs into the hole I'd dug behind me. Slowly and carefully I pushed the soil over the meth, burying the drugs. None of the cops noticed.

When the police had completed a thorough search of my car, they pulled me off the ledge and put me into a different squad car than Jackson.

"We know it's your drug operation," the female cop said. "We know you are a big time drug dealer."

I continued to deny knowing anything about drugs, and finally the cop just sort of gave up and walked away.

The police took us to Jackson's house. They had a search warrant and methodically went all through the house where they found meth pipes, foils and all sorts of evidence of illegal drugs. Later the dog found the plastic bag of meth in the dirt on the ledge, but I insisted that I didn't know anything about it. Jackson was taken to jail, but to my surprise, I was released.

If the police had found all that meth on me, I would surely have been sent to prison for five or six years. The whole incident scared me, but it didn't keep me away from Jackson and our friends. It was more fun to hang out with Jackson and smoke meth than to face the responsibilities at work or worry about a brush with the cops.

I went through the entire $3000 Dad gave me within the first six weeks of being in LA. I knew I would have to support myself, so I looked for another job, when I wasn't getting high with Jackson and our friends. I wasn't worried, because I knew how to take care of myself.

I found a new job at a different salon in Arcadia. It wasn't as glamorous as the job I had before, but it paid enough that I was able to support myself. Jackson and his friends were my family now, and as Christmas approached, I was looking forward to celebrating the holiday as part of his family. But when Christmas arrived, I wasn't invited to Jackson's huge family celebration. Instead, Trent and I had a McDonald's chicken sandwich together on Christmas Day.

When Jackson came back from his family celebration on Christmas Day, we got into my car and went out for a drive. Along the way we saw Trent and his friend Julian at McDonalds. I pulled into the parking lot and Trent and Julian came over to the car. I knew Julian and classified him as a "tweaker" or an annoying pest that hung around looking for ways to gather gossip or be the center of attention.

"Hi!" Trent said, "Can we get a ride?"

"No, you can't have a ride," Jackson answered before I could even open my mouth. The bad blood between Jackson and Trent was still flowing. I'd heard that Jackson had threatened Trent, warning him not to help me during the recent kidnapping. Jackson's jealousy and crazy attitude toward Trent was festering into unreasonable issues.

"Aw, come on," Trent said good naturedly, "Julian and I need a ride home."

"No, you can't have a ride!" Jackson barked. "Erin is dropping me off and she's going to Lauren's house. She's not going to give you a ride."

Trent was looking at me with a gleam that said he knew I'd be back to pick him up in a few minutes, after I took Jackson home. No words were spoken, and I just put the car in reverse and left the parking lot.

I took Jackson back to his house, and said good bye. As he hugged me I whispered, "I love you."

"Don't pick Trent up," Jackson said in slow, deliberate words of warning. "Go straight to Lauren's house. Do not pick him up." He gripped my arms tightly and as I pushed away from him, I could see an evil glint in his eye.

I got in my car and drove directly back to McDonalds. Trent and Julian were still there and came out to the car. Trent got in my car, but I refused to take Julian with me. I told Trent that he could just borrow my car over night. So Trent got into my car and rode with me to Lauren's house, promising Julian that he'd be back to get him in a few minutes. He agreed that he would return with my car the next morning.

When I arrived at Lauren's house, I called Jackson. The first thing he asked me was, "Did you pick up Trent?"

"No," I lied. Trent was sitting next to me in the car as I placed that phone call. Trent left with my car and Lauren and I went into her house, where we spent the night.

When Lauren and I woke up the next morning, Trent was right on time to bring my car back. We were all supposed to meet up at Jackson's house that day, so I decided to take Trent home first, and then go get Jackson, and together he and I would pick up Trent. I thought this would eliminate any jealous concerns that Jackson had about Trent.

So Lauren and I dropped Trent off, and we drove back to Jackson's house. Lauren and I walked into the large marble foyer of Jackson's house and up the staircase to Jackson's room. I was surprised to find Julian there with Jackson. They were both drunk and smoking meth together. This was not good. Julian was not someone I trusted. He had always been more than happy to create conflict.

I took one look at Jackson and I could tell he was seething with anger. "Did you pick up Trent?" He demanded.

"No," I said.

Julian piped up then, in his tweaky voice, "Ah man, are you really going to lie to him?"

Jackson glared at me.

"You're gonna believe that freaking tweaker?!" I demanded. I could feel the fear swell inside of me. Jackson was such a huge man and when he was angry he was a powerful force of brute strength. Adding the meth and the booze to his anger made him dangerous and insane.

Julian and I began screaming at each other, while Jackson sat watching us. Julian enjoyed accusing me and I kept denying all of his charges.

Finally I'd had enough, "Forget this!" I screamed. "I don't have to take this. Lauren, let's go."

I raced out the door, down the stairs with Jackson right behind me. In the foyer, I reached for the door handle with one hand, while I grabbed my shoes with the other. Suddenly from behind me, Jackson picked me up and body-slammed me into the marble floor, the same way a WWF wrestler might hurl an opponent in the professional wrestling ring.

I was numb at first, but then the pain that shot through my hip was intense, sharp and excruciating. I struggled for breath on the floor, stunned.

Lauren and Julian came running down the stairs behind us. Jackson was standing over me, and he raised his arms up, "I didn't do it!" he defended himself to them. "I never touched her."

I was hyperventilating, gasping for air, and I couldn't get up. The pain was burning in my hip socket and I thought surely it had broken when I hit the marble floor.

Lauren leaned over me, "Erin, you have to get up," she whispered. "We have to get out of here. Come on, I'll help you."

I don't know how I got up, because I was hurting so badly I could barely breathe. Lauren pulled me to my feet and she helped me wobble to my car. I had to drag my leg as I was crouched over, gasping in pain.

"Just get in your car," Lauren encouraged me. "Come on, I'll help you. But let's get in the car before he does something else - something worse."

Somehow Lauren got me into my car, and she got in the passenger side and locked the doors. "Just go!" Lauren cried in panic. "Just start the car and let's go!"

I was hunched over the steering wheel, holding my side and crying. "I can't drive," I sobbed. "I think my hip is broken."

"Oh Erin," Lauren started crying too. "I'm so sorry. But I'm scared. We have to get out of here. Just start the car and I'll help you drive. We just have to get out of here!"

Shaking, I turned the key in the ignition and slowly backed out of the driveway. My hip was throbbing and I was shaking in pain and panic. The car crawled down the road as Lauren and I made our escape. I didn't know what was going to happen next, but I was afraid for Trent, and I knew he was waiting for us to pick him up.

In my agony, I drove to Trent's house. Lauren told Trent what Jackson had done to me this time, and Trent was furious at Jackson and fearful for me. Trent called Jackson on the phone and told Jackson he was a coward for hurting a woman and threatened to beat Jackson up before he turned him over to the cops. I was in too much pain to follow the one-sided conversation but I knew there was an intense exchanging of words and Trent was ready to defend me.

Lauren was determined that I needed to go to the emergency room. "We have to go to the hospital, Erin. You could have serious internal injuries."

I didn't want to go to the hospital or to have to explain my injuries to anyone. I just wanted a safe place to rest and recover. So when I refused to go to the hospital Lauren took me to her boyfriend's house, where I crashed in a quiet bedroom.

I checked my hip and it was swollen and a red mark had formed, but the throbbing had subsided and I decided that my injury wasn't as bad as I'd feared. "It's not that bad," I told Lauren. She gave me some Tylenol and I went to sleep.

When I woke up the next morning, I couldn't move. I was in so much pain; I could barely inhale or exhale. I didn't know what to do. I was in a level of pain I'd never experienced before. When I looked at my hip, I was astonished to find that I had a bruise the size of a football. It looked like a sunset with bright red, purple, yellow, blue and hot pink streaks shooting out from the center.

Lauren took one look at my bruise and she insisted that I go to the hospital. "I've never seen anything that looked like that!" she exclaimed.

"Oh my god!" Trent gasped when he saw my bruise. "Lauren's right, you have to be treated at the hospital."

As much as I wanted medical treatment, I didn't want to have to explain this to anyone. Again I declined going to the hospital, so Lauren loaded me into my car and Trent drove us to her house. Lauren's mother took one look at me and said, "Let's go." And I was off to the hospital.

The emergency room personnel were great. They put me into a bed, took x-rays and ran some tests. I was evaluated for four hours. Everyone kept asking the same question, "How did this happen?"

When I was ready for discharge, a social worker turned up and told me that California law required the hospital to report my injuries as an assault. A crime had been committed against me, and in the state of California domestic violence is not an optional charge. Jackson would be arrested for what he'd done to me.

Dang! This is just what I didn't want to do. I didn't want to report the assault, I didn't want to press charges, and I didn't want to answer any questions.

"Can't we just say I fell?" I asked. I'm not sure if I was protecting myself or Jackson with that question, but I really didn't want the cops involved in this.

"No," the social worker explained, "It has to be reported."

I sighed, resigned to the rules, but I just thought they would report it. I wasn't prepared for the two cops who came to my room. They took my statement and Lauren was there to corroborate my story. She also reminded me of the first time Jackson beat me up, when he took my car keys and left me stranded in the hills.

After the police were satisfied that they knew what had happened, they asked to see my injuries. I started with the little stuff, a scratch here, a bruise there and I lifted my shirt to show them. They took pictures, and then Lauren insisted that I show them the bruise.

When I revealed the bruise on my hip, both officers were speechless for a moment. Then the one asked incredulously, "He did this to you?"

"Yeah," I admitted sheepishly. I was embarrassed that I had suffered from the hand of my boyfriend.

The officer patted my hand, "I've never seen a bruise like that," she said shaking her head. She looked at her partner as she put her camera away and tucked her notebook into her bag.

"We're going to personally arrest him," she said. "I want to make sure this guy understands that what he's done is not okay."

The two police officers went straight to Jackson's house and arrested him. He was booked and put in jail, but he made bail that night. His mother worked in the legal profession and she knew how to get him out of jail quickly.

That night I began to think that maybe I should leave Los Angeles and go back home to Northern California where my family lived. Maybe this life of drugs and lies wasn't as cool as I had thought it was. Maybe I needed to find a safe refuge and a life untainted by drugs. I kept wondering… how did I get to this sad, scary place in my life?

CHAPTER 2

GROWING UP ON THE DELTA

I grew up on the water. My childhood was fun, lively, safe and secure. Mom and Dad enjoyed water sports and I went on my first boating experience at five months old. My parents loved boating and early on I learned to love it too. Growing up in Stockton, California, my childhood offered me countless opportunities to play on the delta, the confluence of the Sacramento and San Joaquin rivers, just east of where these rivers enter Suisun Bay (an upper arm of San Francisco Bay). As a kindergartener, I took swimming lessons and Mom and Dad both had strict water safety rules. Soon I was tubing behind the ski boat and by age seven I was water skiing. Mom and Dad bought a houseboat and we spent every single weekend on the delta. It was always good quality time with my mom, dad and my little sister, Erica.

Nothing was ever more fun than the delta Fourth of July celebration. Erica and I had lots of friends on the water and the fireworks show was our family's favorite event. The pyrotechnic show over the water was amazing, with over 50,000 people and boats everywhere. I remember crazy water fights and laughing all day, eagerly awaiting the show. It was amazing to watch the fireworks explode over the water, with vibrant colors spraying the sky with sparkle. Erica and I would snuggle with

Mom and Dad and I just remember feeling so safe and loved. Today, the fourth of July remains my favorite childhood memory.

As Erica and I grew up, Mom and Dad sold the houseboat and upgraded to a 50-foot yacht. It had two bedrooms and two bathrooms, and the delta was the definite destination each week. Mom and Dad were both very hardworking and I'm grateful that they taught me a strong work ethic early in my life. Dad worked as a project manager, for a furniture installation company. Mom also held a full-time job as a sales rep for a flooring company. My parents were excellent providers for our family, both making good money. Erica and I never had anything less than what we wanted, and usually much more than we asked for. There was always good food on the table, in a very comfortable house, in a safe, well-groomed neighborhood. Our large home was always clean with upgrades throughout. Mom and Dad took pride in our home and kept it well maintained, often upgrading or redecorating with top of the line products.

I tried gymnastics in kindergarten, but after a scary accident that landed me in the emergency room, I gave that up for dance. Dancing became my passion. I started formal dance classes at a studio at age seven and instantly I loved it. I loved being a performer and the sparkly costumes and makeup just added to the glamour of dance for me. I was always kind of wild and crazy about dancing for my family and whenever I danced, I sort of felt like my personality could bubble up outside of my body and fill up the whole stage.

When I was about nine, my mom started taking Erica and me to a Presbyterian church. We went on Sunday morning to Bible study, and then a worship service. I loved the youth group that met on Sunday nights. We played basketball and lots of outdoor activities. I had a lot of fun in that. The church was a very traditional building with beautiful stained glass windows, an altar and all the trappings of religion.

Mom would have Erica and me all dressed up to go to church. I had to sit still in the pews and listen to prayers and lectures I didn't understand. I remember the organ music, standing up and singing weird songs out of a big book, not to God, but to the organ. It was so hard to sit still and listen to the minister talk about boring topics. I yearned for the closing hymn which meant we could go home and get out of the Sunday clothes.

We attended church regularly for about a year. I didn't mind the youth group or the Bible study, but I dreaded the worship service. I would always find my mind wandering to the delta where I knew my dad was having great fun on the water without me.

I was baptized at this church, but I don't remember getting a Bible. Church was about church, not God. I know I heard lots of messages that would have been good for me but I didn't develop any kind of relationship with God. Then one day, with no explanation, we just stopped going to church. I asked Mom about it, but she sort of evaded the question and suddenly we went from attending church every week to not going at all. I didn't mourn the loss; I celebrated because now we were back on the delta with the whole family enjoying life on the river again.

By junior high I was dancing six days a week and by high school I was in a dance physical education class and also competing on a competition dance team through a private dance studio. My competition team thought of ourselves as "hard core" dancers at that point, with six hour practices and expensive uniforms and costumes. My mom chauffeured our team all over, loading up her SUV with giggling girls, loads of luggage and crazy costumes, staying in hotels and cheering me on. She would drive me to the studio for rehearsals and come back five or six hours later to pick me up. Mom and Dad were always so supportive of my dancing.

With all the dancing, I was rail thin. I was a late bloomer to begin with and very petite. I ate heartily and danced with equal energy. I made great friends on the dance team and the structure of the team was very good for me. We'd go to practice and then do homework together between classes. There was little time for anything other than school, homework and dance - and that suited me. All that rehearsing paid off, as our team qualified to compete in Nationals in Los Angeles. Once again Mom loaded up the car with me and a bunch of other dance teammates and rented a hotel room for us, helped us prepare, rehearse and cheered us on as we competed. It's a wonderful memory.

One of my most memorable birthdays was when I turned 16. All at once, I got my driver's license and a shiny almost-brand-new 1996 Honda

Civic. It was white, with a stick shift. Dad tried to teach me how to drive the stick but he nearly had a heart attack as I scratched the gears. Mom had to teach me the basics of using the clutch and coordinating the shifting and brakes, and then after Dad calmed down he took me back out for behind-the-wheel lessons. I loved that car and the freedom it gave me.

CHAPTER 3

TEENAGE ANGST CHARTS A NEW COURSE

*E*rica and I were the best of friends when we were children. She was three years behind me and I adored her. One of the worst losses I suffered from my addiction was the loss of my sister's respect. I loved being the big sister to Erica, but as my life began to spin out of control during high school our sister confidences turned from Erica looking up to me, to Erica trying to learn my obvious mistakes.

When I was 13 I started going to work with my dad. I worked as the furniture installation company's summer receptionist, and office assistant. I learned office protocol and helped out by answering the phone and filing. By the time I was 15, I landed my first real paying job as a hostess at Marie Calendar's Restaurant. This changed my plans for the weekends because now I had responsibilities at my job and couldn't spend every Saturday and Sunday on the delta. Mom would often stay home with me, but I was 15 and capable of staying by myself, and before long, I convinced her to go on to the fun at the delta and let me take care of things at home by myself.

Mom and Dad were cautious about leaving me alone on the weekend and set strict standards for where I could be and who I could be with. Mom required that the minute I got home from work on Saturday night that I would call her. Dutifully, I always did. I'd call Mom on the delta and we'd chat about our days. Then I'd say good night and tell her I was going to bed. As soon as I hung up the phone, I took off with friends to hang out all night. That was the summer when I started smoking marijuana.

I think I was in the eighth grade the first time I went to a teen alcohol party. The first time I drank alcohol was my freshman year. And I will always remember the first time I got drunk. I was a sophomore and it was a life-changing event.

It was just two weeks before my 16th birthday. I was hanging out with a few friends at an unsupervised party and some older guys showed up. We started drinking Jose Cuervo and we did shots all night. I had no idea what tequila would do to me, and with the encouragement of everyone, I kept drinking until I was completely hammered. I lost my virginity that night, and unlike I had promised myself for as long as I could remember, it wasn't special, it wasn't romantic, it wasn't with my soul mate who loved me. Worst of all, I didn't even remember it. I was so upset the next morning when I realized what I had done, and even today I still grieve for that loss of innocence and wish that I could take it back. I know that without the fog of alcohol clouding my mind and judgment, that would never have happened, and I will always live with that regret.

Experiencing that blackout really scared me. I vowed to never drink again. But a month later, I was back at the parties, joining all the reckless behavior of alcohol and marijuana. By this time I was dating Brandon, a high school "bad boy," a year older than I was, but in the same grade. This gave me a sort of protection, since no one wanted to cross Brandon. Brandon hung out with a crowd of people who were older than he was, so my social world expanded to include many people who were in their 20's, who didn't go to school and lived a dangerous lifestyle.

At that time of my life, binge drinking didn't seem unusual or risky. Binge drinking was just me dabbling in the adult world party scene. It seemed normal to me. Mom and Dad had alcohol in the house when I was growing up. They were both successful and stable, so I didn't think of alcohol as anything bad. I looked around at my friends, and drinking yourself sick was what everyone did. Parties were peppered with various kinds of beer, wine, hard liquor or whatever anyone brought and we were just having fun. I thought it was normal to drink, get hammered and play around with drugs. Everyone smoked a little marijuana. We weren't bad, we weren't addicts and we weren't unstable. We were just fun-loving kids, looking for a good time.

I did all the normal high school activities besides partying. I took Brandon to the Sadie's dance, and he took me to the prom. Brandon played on the football team and I went to all the games. My friends and I made T shirts for the games, or special events. I danced with a P.E. dance class and we did a lot of performances at school.

Our house was always full of my friends when I was growing up. Mom and Dad enjoyed having a house full of girls and we were the destination sleepover house. Now with both parents out of the house overnight, I kept that tradition and became the hostess for unsupervised parties, stealing alcohol and offering a haven for wild crowds. Most Sundays I would spend all morning cleaning up all the mess, hoping that Mom and Dad wouldn't notice anything out of the ordinary when they returned Sunday night from the river.

One Saturday night things got really crazy at my party and kids who were a lot older than I showed up. There was a lot of liquor, kegs of beer and plenty of marijuana. There were kids in every room of the house, engaging in one stage of partying or another. My dad had a huge, expensive sound system, and the guys had it blaring away all night. I woke up that next morning to find three empty kegs lying in the back yard and a huge mess. I cleaned all day, trying to hide all the evidence of the party but when Mom and Dad got home I had a lot of explaining to do. Things had been broken and Erica's Lakers jersey had been stolen. When Mom went to the freezer to get the ice cream she found two 40 ounce bottles of beer.

"Erin," Mom called to me. "What are these? What is this?"

I played dumb. "I don't know." It was the truth. I hadn't put those bottles in the freezer.

"How can you not know where this came from?" Dad asked me. "We don't drink 40 ounce bottles of beer. These are not ours." The bottles had exploded in the freezer when the beer froze and Mom was trying to clean it up as Dad wanted answers.

Then things hit the fan. There was no defense for what I had done, and

Mom and Dad grounded me for six months. I was allowed to go to school, work, and home. I was still allowed to dance with the dance team and I was grateful that they let me keep my job. For a few weeks Mom stayed home on the weekends so that I was supervised after work. After a month or so, Mom went back to the delta to be with Dad. She left me with a whole list of rules. I'd nod my head, and promise to go to work and come straight home. And I did keep my promise by going to work; but then I would come home with plenty of time to hold a big party all night.

By the end of sophomore year, Mom and Dad decided to take me out of my dance classes because my grades were dropping. Their thinking was that it would give me more time to study. Instead, it took me out of the structure and discipline of the dance studio and I went crazy.

The beginning of junior year, I started cutting classes and skipping school. One morning, the second week of school, I drove to Brandon's house to pick him up for school. When I walked into the house, I found a whole bunch of Brandon's friends sitting around smoking marijuana.

"What's up, guys?" I asked.

"Hey, Erin!" Brandon greeted me. "We decided not to go to first and second period today. We're going to go to school at brunch. Want to stay here with us?"

It didn't take much to talk me into skipping school. "Sure," I said, and plopped down on the couch.

We had to time the arrival at school just as the brunch bell rang, so we wouldn't get caught cutting class. Brandon lived close enough to the school that we could hear the dismissal bell, so we were watching the clock and listening for the bell. Right before it was time to go, one of the guys pulled out more marijuana and they all decided to smoke a bit more before we left. I was the only one in the group who hadn't smoked marijuana all morning.

I sighed, took my purse off my shoulder and sat back down. "We want to get there when the crowd is out for brunch," I reminded them. A few more minutes wouldn't matter.

"We're cool," they all nodded, passing the marijuana around between them. When they got to me I declined. I don't know why, but when it was my turn I passed it off, "I'm good."

"Come on," one of Brandon's friends encouraged me.

"No, I don't feel like it," I said kindly. "Thanks, but I'm good."

So all of the guys smoked marijuana and then they all piled into my car and we drove over to campus. We arrived just a few seconds early. As we walked onto campus, we realized that the bell hadn't rung yet and students were all still in class. As we came around the end of the gym all the deans were standing right there.

Dang! We were busted.

"Let's go," the deans said. We had all cut school so many times, and our discipline files were so full, that they knew who we were immediately.

We were escorted to the office and the school resource police officer came and drug tested all of us. Everyone tested positive for marijuana, except me. All the guys were expelled for coming to campus under the influence of drugs.

The school counselor and the dean called my parents and Mom came down to school. Everyone seemed to be in my business at that point, telling me that I shouldn't be dating Brandon or hanging out with all his friends. The counselor even told my mom not to let me date Brandon.

My parents were so angry. Mom went from tears of disappointment to tears of fury as she tried to figure out what would put me back on the right track. She asked my counselor, "What do we do with her?" pointing out that they had already grounded me, taken away my dance classes, and all my other privileges.

This time Mom and Dad took my car away and I had to take the bus to school. After having the freedom and style of my own classy transportation, this was a big dent to my ego. I was forbidden to see Brandon, and since he was expelled from my school, I couldn't see him at school either. This punishment I didn't stop me from dating him. We stayed in touch through phone calls and notes, and after a month or so, Mom and Dad let him come over to the house to see me.

Before long, Mom and Dad started to trust me again. They thought I was seeing the error of my ways and getting back on a track of success. But in reality I went to class when I wanted to, cut classes I could get away with, and even took vodka in water bottles to class.

Of course, my grades plummeted, but it didn't matter. High school was fun; I worked and partied all the time. In our community it was common for kids to throw "orchard parties" out in the rural farmland, bringing a keg of beer, lots of booze and throwing a party on private property among the peach trees. I prided myself in being a "wild child" and if there was a party going on, I wanted to be there. I continued to date Brandon and we partied together all the time.

By senior year, I hadn't made any of the plans most seniors do. I was in the AVID class, which provides support for students headed toward a four-year college, but I had no real plans after high school. I took the SATs but I didn't do well on them. I was contemplating going to college, but I couldn't decide if I wanted to start at a junior college or go directly to a four-year university. School was not my thing, but I had done well enough that I was accepted into California State University Stanislaus. My senior schedule had six periods but I never went to more than two periods a day. The rest of the time I smoked marijuana, drank alcohol and got high.

By mid-senior year, I had completed all the requirements for graduation at East Union High. However the school had rules about clearing discipline detention hours to be allowed to walk in the graduation ceremony. I was shocked one day when I was called to the principal's office.

"Erin," my principal said. "You can't walk in your graduation ceremony unless you clear all your detention hours."

"Okay," I said. "How many do I need to clear?"

"Over 1000," my principal calmly said. I was through the kindness of my counselor, that I was able to work off all those detention hours and still participate in my high school graduation ceremony.

CHAPTER 4

LIFE AFTER GRADUATION

*H*igh school graduation was a milestone in my life that I barely celebrated. I walked in the graduation ceremony from East Union High, but I didn't participate in any of the graduation trips or celebrations. I looked at graduation as the end of high school and the beginning of my life as an independent, wild, party girl.

Brandon and I had been dating for over two years and the first thing I did that summer was break up with him. It wasn't because he had done anything wrong or that I had found someone I liked better. I was just ready to move on.

Brandon was extremely upset and angry with me. He and I had been very serious about our relationship and had even talked about being married. We'd made long-range plans about living our lives together and had enjoyed a really good relationship. I really don't know what prompted me to break up with him but that summer I truly did complete my mission and I went out nearly every night to party.

I had a job working at a major department store in the mall and I enjoyed hanging out with a lot of the girls and guys who worked there. They were a fun group and we were hard core partiers. When the mall closed, we used to drive to Sacramento or San Francisco to go to different clubs or parties. That summer I was out every single night - partying.

My main drug of choice at that time was alcohol. I was drinking like a fish. My two favorite drinks were Captain Morgan and Southern Comfort, but when I was at the bar I drank Long Islands.

Even though I wasn't 21, I had a fake ID and I never had trouble being served. Our whole crowd was completely irresponsible about driving with alcohol and more than once I drove drunk. Often I'd have diet cola and Southern Comfort blended in a bottle and drank it as I drove up the freeway.

I remember one night, driving through a McDonalds drive-thru on our way to a Sacramento night club. After we paid for our meal, I pulled away from the window but misjudged the curve of the exit. I was so hammered; I drove over the curb and down the landscaped hill. I jumped the curb and ended up at the bottom of the hill. Two friends were in the car with me and none of us were a bit concerned about the damage to the car, but instead, we worried about the jumbled French fries and spilled soda. We all laughed ourselves silly and the continued on our way to the party.

I had no real plans after high school. Even though I'd been accepted at a well respected university near my home, I knew that I wasn't a "school person." With no specific collegiate goals, there was no way I wanted to enroll in college.

In July, I decided to try cosmetology school. A new, highly ranked school had just opened in Stockton and I was accepted there. Getting a cosmetology license requires 1600 hours of study, plus passing the California State Boards. Two of my friends from high school also enrolled and the three of us were excited to begin studying for a career that would give us skills to be able to support ourselves. I started cosmetology school in July going to class Tuesday through Saturday from 9 a.m. to 5 p.m. each day. I quit my job at the department store and landed a great job at Luxx, a high end fashion store in the Stockton Mall.

While I was at cosmetology school I met a girl named Elaine who went to school on the same schedule as I did, and she also worked at Luxx. I also met a really cute guy named James at Luxx and soon Elaine, James and I became great friends and were regular partying buddies. We'd go to school, then to work, and then out to clubs, bars or private parties several nights a week. We were like the three musketeers, always hanging out together, always looking for the next place to have fun.

Within a year, I was the first of my friends to graduate in my cosmetology class. I took my State Boards and passed my first time. I took a certain amount of pride in this accomplishment because a lot of the girls took the exam but didn't pass. I started my career as a stylist at a salon in Modesto called Salon Diego Julio, assisting the owner and working as a receptionist.

Mom and Dad had moved to Modesto, about 30 miles south of Stockton. Even though I was still working at Luxx in Stockton, I was happy to get a job as a stylist closer to home in Modesto.

About that time, the manager at Luxx quit and opened a restaurant in Stockton and she hired me to work there too. So now that I was finished with school, I took on a third job; working at the salon in Modesto, at Luxx and now at the restaurant, both in Stockton. I was super busy all the time, making a lot of money for a young person and since I was working two out of three jobs in Stockton, I ended up staying overnight in Stockton often, usually staying at Elaine's house.

Up until I met Elaine, I smoked a lot of marijuana, drank a whole lot of alcohol and dabbled in cocaine. But I had only tried meth once. It was when I was in high school and I had asked Brandon about it. Brandon did not want me to try meth and warned me that it was extremely addictive and that people often became addicted to meth very quickly.

I kept pestering Brandon about just trying meth and finally one day he gave in. "Erin," Brandon told me very sternly. "I'll let you try it once, with me. But that's it. It's super addictive. You're never going to do it again, okay?"

I agreed and Brandon showed me how to smoke meth off of a piece of foil.

I vividly remember that first sensation of meth. It was a powerful aura that overwhelmed me. It clearly was a potent substance and it didn't make me feel good or excited about it - it scared me and made me very uncomfortable. Brandon made me promise that I would never try it again, and I didn't think I would.

Now a few years later, and a much more seasoned party girl, I was always up for anything exciting. Elaine and I were using and abusing lots of different drugs, and we decided that we wanted to lose weight. Looking back, this was ridiculous, because I have always been very petite and thin. But Elaine was always focused on weight loss and I joined her goal. We were working out together at 5 a.m. with a personal trainer five days a week, trying to get in shape, but not getting the results we wanted. We tried several diets, and started taking diet pills that contained ephedra which made me feel jittery all the time.

Fixated on losing weight, Elaine and I agreed that we could use a little more help. We had both heard that meth was a great weight loss aid. After researching meth on-line and its potential to help with weight loss, Elaine and I thought we'd give it a try. We found somebody who would sell us meth, but then we had a problem. We didn't know how to use it. First Elaine and I tried to snort it. Then we did more research and figured out how to free base it the way Brandon had shown me years before, off of a little piece of aluminum foil.

Free basing meth takes some practice. The meth crystals are placed on the foil and then a flame is placed beneath the foil. As the meth crystals get hot, they begin to melt and you have to take a straw and suck in the toxic fumes for the high.

The meth smoke and fumes are not only toxic, they are hot and liquid. If you suck it in too quickly it goes into your throat and crystallizes and a hot liquid sticks in your throat. It burns with incredible pain. It can also crystallize in your lungs, resulting in instant death.

Despite the dangerous, complicated technique, in no time I came to be proficient in meth smoking and looking forward to my next chance to use it with every breath. Since I was working all three jobs, I remember going from job to job, planning how to find time for my next dose of meth. It gave me such incredible energy!

The restaurant where I worked was down on the Stockton waterfront, and there was a big, empty field along the route to get there. Elaine and I would pull over in that remote area and smoke meth coming or going to work. I'd go to the salon to work and then drive back to pick up Elaine and together we'd drive out to work at restaurant. I'd change my clothes in the car out there near that big empty field and before heading off to work, we'd smoke meth with our heads down below the windows in case anyone drove by. After our shifts at the restaurant, Elaine and I would go out partying and then back to her house for the night.

Eventually, Elaine and I decided to get our own place. So she moved out of her parents' house and together we rented a tiny, old, one-bedroom house in old town Stockton.

This was the beginning of a very bad time for me. Elaine and I were doing a lot of meth, coming and going to our different jobs. One night, my little sister, Erica spent the night at our little house. Erica found meth pipes in the shower and meth in the bathroom. Trying to help me, she went home and told Mom and Dad.

Throughout my teens, there had often been tension between me and my dad. He had addiction issues of his own, and I had grown up watching my dad drink too much alcohol regularly. As I grew out of my childhood, Dad and I butted heads a lot. He always tried to control everyone and everything around him. Mom and Erica tried to make him happy and do whatever he wanted. But I was different. I refused to be pushed around and I did whatever I wanted, despite his objections. During high school, our dinner table was not pleasant. After my dad had his third drink in the evening, he'd turn angry and mean-spirited. He'd yell and Mom and Erica would take it. I'd yell back.

My sad relationship with my father contributed to the tension between him and my mother. I vividly remember my dad telling my mom one time, "Pick me or pick Erin. I'm leaving or she's leaving."

With my meth use on the forefront of the family focus, I could see Mom and Dad trying to find balance within our family, even if their marriage was on the rocks. I was also aware that the relationship that I treasured with my little sister, Erica was on shaky ground. I was no longer her role model, and instead someone she was advised to observe to avoid major mistakes.

Overall, this was a really bad time for me and my family. Mom and Dad were almost ready to divorce, I was a meth addict and my sweet little sister, Erica – the perfect beautiful child, with the 4.0 grade point average - was being overshadowed by all that spun around me and my problems.

Mom called a few days after Erica had stayed over night with me and said that she and Dad wanted to talk to me. So, unceremoniously, Mom, Dad and Erica held their own intervention. At first all three of them began to talk about how my drug use affected them and why they wanted me to stop. I didn't want to hear it, so I got up and stormed into the bedroom.

Mom followed me and she tried to talk to me about using meth. I started crying and insisted that I wasn't using drugs. Things were complicated because Elaine and I were having a big fight at the time, and Elaine had decided to move back in with her mother. I couldn't afford the little house on my own and now with Mom and Dad upset over my drug use, I didn't have any option of moving back home with them.

I kept insisting that I wasn't using drugs, but I had no explanation for what Erica had found. Dad was so mad, he finally just said, "Okay, we're out of here." And they all left.

With Elaine no longer willing to be my roommate, I begged to move back home. Mom and Dad agreed, but only if I promised to stop using meth. With all sincerity, I pledged to stop using drugs and to get back on track with my life.

It was all just a sham. I continued to smoke meth in my shower and pretended to sleep like a normal person by being as quiet as possible in my room all night. Often I'd be scrapbooking, cleaning or playing on the computer long past 3 a.m.

My bedroom shared a bathroom with Erica's room and there were dividing doors for the shower and toilet. It was a perfect way for me to hide my meth use, by simply hiding away in either the shower or toilet section of the common bath to light up.

But my parents are not stupid, and Mom and Dad knew things were not right. When Mom found me in the toilet area of the bathroom pretending to dry my hair, she knew I was using. In no uncertain terms, I was told that I had to move out.

Mom told me to pack what I could get in my car and leave. She would not allow drugs in her house or around my sister. The day I moved out, I was high. As I prepared to leave she asked me, "Erin, is this how you plan to live your life?"

"What do you mean?" I asked innocently.

"Is this – using drugs, lying, sneaking around - is this how you plan to live the rest of your life?"

"Yep," I told her, looking her directly in the eye. "It's working for me. I'm good with this."

I shocked my mother with that attitude, but I really thought it was working for me. I had three jobs, endless energy and I loved smoking meth. It was my reason for getting up in the morning. I wasn't sick, and the drugs had changed my perspective and values so much, that I didn't see that I was losing anything by choosing to use meth over my family.

I moved in with Brandon's sister. Brandon and I started to rekindle our relationship, and sort of dating again. By then James had moved to LA, and all I could think about was moving to Los Angeles too. With my cosmetology license, I wanted to get a job doing hair and makeup for Hollywood high fashion photo shoots and runway shows.

I paid Brandon's sister rent to live in her home with her family. When Brandon found out I was saving my money and working as much overtime as I could so that I could move to Los Angeles, Brandon was so mad! He promised me the world, if I'd just stay right there in Manteca with him.

"I'll buy you a house," Brandon told me. "Or I'll buy you a new car. Just please, don't go to LA. Stay here with me."

I lived with Brandon's sister and her family for three months before she discovered that I was doing drugs. One day she confronted me, "I know you're doing meth, Erin," she said softly. "I can't have that around my kids. You have to leave."

Mom and Dad had separated and Mom agreed to let me move back in with her. Every weekend, for the next month and a half, I drove to Los Angeles, preparing to make the move. It's a six hour drive from Manteca, but I could get there in four hours.

Mom went with me one weekend and paid for us to stay in a nice hotel while I went to some interviews at a few salons.

Erin's mother, Lisa remembers it this way.

Erin had some interviews, but she wasn't focused on them. I watched her get ready and it seemed like a waste of time and money to me. She was supposed to be down there looking for a job and a place to live, but all she seemed to really want was to connect with someone who could link her to drugs.

Without drugs, Erin is focused and organized. But the girl I saw trying to move to Los Angeles was flighty, almost squirrely and it was so frustrating to see all her potential wasted by the drug that she so obviously craved.

When we got back from that trip, I decided that I was definitely going to Los Angeles. Dad had moved to Oregon, and I decided to ask him to help me financially. Dad agreed to give me $3000 to get my start in Los Angeles. I wanted cash, but Mom and Dad insisted on giving me traveler's checks instead.

Lisa recalls this as the beginning of her nightmare.

I didn't want to give Erin money, because I was afraid she'd just spend it all on drugs. But her father wanted to help her get her professional career started, so he gave her $3000. Just as I feared Erin began to misuse the funds she was given. In one pre-moving trip to Los Angeles, Erin blew $500 in one weekend.

She had come back home to gather more of her things, and I remember her waking me up in the night, angry and short with me, because she had lost what was left of her traveler's checks. Erin was either high or coming down from being high and she was tearing the room apart. I got on the phone with AMEX to file a claim. Erin was nasty to the person on the AMEX phone and couldn't understand why we had to file a claim; she just wanted them to give her new checks. It took a few days, but I was able to have the traveler's checks replaced, and she left with the money her father wanted her to have.

Later, after Erin had completely moved out and I did deep cleaning in her room, I found $2500 in traveler's checks, along with meth foils, crystals and other drug paraphernalia.

CHAPTER 5

RUNNING FOR MY LIFE

At first, Los Angeles was all I had hoped for. I was thrilled to be living in the "City of Angels," and working at a famous hotel as a stylist for the Hollywood elite. This was the dream job, with all the glamour and glitz of a celebrity lifestyle. Life in Los Angeles was great - for awhile. Jackson's way of life was exciting, edgy and exactly what I had been craving. But when I lost my glamorous job, and I began to focus on the drug culture instead, I was unprepared for the volatile and violent consequences of dating a drug dealer.

Even though Jackson had been arrested for smashing me into the marble floor, he made bail the same day. I was certain that he was capable of more violence and it scared me. Then, as I recovered from being beaten, Jackson broke into my car. He left it inoperable, parked in a parking lot somewhere in Los Angeles.

My life was scrambled up and my world turned upside down. Besides my car trouble, I'd lost my job, half of my stuff was lost when Jackson scattered it in the street, and this person I loved had physically abused me and threatened to kill me. I didn't know what to do, where to go, or how to plan the next day.

I gathered the courage to call my mom. I was relieved that she answered the phone, but disappointed to learn that she wasn't able to help me. Mom had just gotten off of an airplane and was in Florida at a business conference. She would be there for at least three days. Mom listened to my story kindly, but reminded me that she couldn't help because she wasn't even on the west coast. She told me to call Dad.

So I hung up the phone and tried to muster the courage to call my dad to carefully broach the subject of coming home.

"Dad," I said slowly. "My life is screwed up. My boyfriend just beat me up twice in a couple of weeks. They arrested him, but he got out right away. He's threatened to kill me. My car is broken and I don't know if it's safe for me to stay here in LA."

Dad was cautiously sympathetic. He didn't give me a direct answer. Instead, he asked some questions and I answered them, giving him the drama of what happened, but no information about the drugs involved. "Your mother is in Florida, at a sales conference. I'll talk with her and call you back."

I didn't know what Mom would say. Both Mom and Dad had been disappointed in my decisions and the consequences of my lifestyle over and over again. I'd lied to them and taken advantage of their love in countless ways. I'd abandoned most of the values they had taught me, and I'd been very disrespectful to them whenever they challenged my choices. I didn't know if they would welcome me home or not, and I couldn't imagine the conversation between them. I didn't really think that either of them would be happy or excited about me coming home.

My mom remembers the conversation well.

Erin's mother - Lisa

I was standing in the baggage area of the airport when Erin called. As soon as I hung up the phone from talking with Erin, I called her father, Mike. I told him that she would be calling. I was so disappointed in the life Erin had chosen. I knew that I could not continue to bail her out if I wanted her to change. I was exhausted from dealing with all of Erin's drama. I felt "done" with it. I loved my daughter, but this young woman who continued to make choices that revolved around drugs instead of family and love, wasn't my daughter anymore. I didn't want her back home.

By the time Erin connected with her dad and by the time I arrived at my hotel, Mike called me. I stepped outside the hotel room and sat down on the floor in the hall, bracing myself for yet another problem with my oldest daughter.

"I think we have to do something," Mike said. "The boyfriend beat her up badly enough to put her in the hospital. The police arrested him, but he's already out on bail. Lisa, I think we are going to have to help her. I don't want her to end up dead."

"Oh Mike," I began to cry. "I don't want her at home. But what if he comes after her in retaliation for the arrest? Next time he really might kill her." There were several emotions swirling around inside of me. I did not want to be involved with any more of Erin's drug consequences. I didn't know what to feel about the situation. I really had resigned myself that I was done with my daughter.

"You're right," Mike said matter-of-factly. "I don't want her to come home either. In this situation I think bringing her home is the right thing to do." Mike paused, and then continued, "I didn't want to just tell her she could come home without talking with you first."

"I really don't want her to come home," I said honestly to Mike. "I'm so tired of her lies, and what the drugs have changed her into."

Mike sighed on the other end of the line. "Lisa, I love her too. But when do we stop helping her? What good does it do when we help her? It never causes her to change. She's still on drugs. Hell, I bet she's on drugs now, waiting for us to call her back. I want this to be over too. But I want to do the right thing."

The tears were rolling down my cheeks. I shared my husband's frustration. We both felt that we had lost our daughter. "I know." I agreed. "I don't want her to come home with all her lies and drugs. But what will happen if we don't help her?"

"He might kill her," Mike said flatly, without emotion. "As much as I don't want to be part of Erin's drama, I'm not sure that we have a choice. It's a very real possibility that after he was arrested he may just decide to finish what he started in retaliation. What do you think?"

I knew Mike was right. "I don't think we have a choice," I said with resignation. "He really might kill her next time."

Dad called me back within a couple of hours. He asked me for the street address of where I was. "I'm coming to get you tomorrow," Dad said. "Where is your car?"

"In a parking lot," I told him.

Dad said, "Good. I'll be there at 10 a.m. tomorrow. Be ready."

I started to cry with relief.

The next morning Dad left Modesto at 4:30 a.m. He came to get me first, and then we rented a trailer to tow my car home. We located my car in a parking lot in Pasadena, loaded it on the trailer and I was back home in Modesto by 6 p.m. that night.

I felt so much relief, being back home. I was determined that this was going to be a fresh start for me. I was done doing drugs, done with people who used drugs, done with abusive relationships. I would start over.

"Thanks, Dad," I hugged my father that night. "My life is going to be good from now on. I promise."

And it was - for a couple weeks. First, I got my job back at Luxx with a promotion. I really liked the interim manager there, a girl named Amanda. I liked her even better when I found out that she used meth. Since my car wasn't repaired yet, Amanda offered to let me stay at her house and together we commuted to Stockton for work. I thought this was a great plan, since it saved my parents driving me the 30 miles from Modesto to Stockton each day. But Mom and Dad thought it was disrespectful to them and their offer to help me regain my life. It also tipped them off that I had broken my promise and that I was back using meth.

I was so glad to be back on meth; so happy to feel the power of the drug take hold of my energy. Even on drugs, I was still trying to rebuild my relationship with my parents and they were trying to help me rebuild my life.

One night, after smoking meth with Amanda, I spent the whole night cleaning the house because I was too high from meth to sleep. About 6 a.m. I crashed into unconsciousness unable to wake up even with the phone ringing in my ear when Mom called to find out why I was late to meet them. Mom and Dad drove to Amanda's house and pounded on the door and even the window of my room, trying to get me to wake up. Unable to rouse me, they knew for sure that I'd lied again.

I came home to a confrontation with Mom, "You've got to get out," she told me. That was fine with me. I moved into Amanda's apartment permanently with Amanda and her two pre-school age sons.

It was a great arrangement. We worked about 70 hours a week; Amanda was the manager and I was the sales lead, assistant manager. We went to work together, spent our days trying to make corporate sales goals and quotas, then returning home to party most of the night. We were great friends, making a lot of money and spending most of it on drugs.

Amanda's parents built a new house on their rural property and Amanda was invited to move into the original farm house out there. Soon Amanda and I were fixing up that old house, decorating the boys' rooms and settling in. Jackson and I reconciled, and I sent him bus tickets to visit each month. Amanda couldn't stand Jackson, but I rationalized having him back in my life, pointing out to Amanda that Jackson was helping us fix up her house.

Amanda hired her old boyfriend, Randall to tile the floors in the farm house, and before long, they were dating again. Randall was also heavily involved with drugs, and soon our house became the "kick it" spot. Everyone brought their friends over to our house to do drugs.

My arrangement with Amanda was that in exchange for rent, I was the nanny and housekeeper. I loved having a clean house, and enjoyed looking after Amanda's boys. I thrived on being the homemaker and nanny in our arrangement.

One night Amanda told me that Randall was coming for dinner. "Okay, cool." I told her as I was tossing the salad. But I could tell there was more for her to tell me. "What's up?" I asked.

Amanda sighed, "Well, he's bringing this friend who just got out of prison."

I didn't say anything, but I'm sure the look I gave her revealed my dismay. Amanda continued, "Don't say anything, okay?"

"Okay," I nodded, and planned for one more person for dinner.

When Randall and his friend, Emilio, the ex-con arrived, I found Emilio to be very polite. He was handsome in a rugged sort of way; tough looking, with tattoos and scars. He wasn't like anyone I'd ever met before. He introduced himself and we had a nice time over dinner with Amanda, Randall and her little boys. It was after Amanda and I put the boys to bed, that I found out what was really different about Emilio.

We were sitting around, visiting when Emilio opened his coat and pulled out a Tupperware container full of meth. My jaw hit the floor. I had never seen that much meth at one time before. It was probably a pound of the delightful crystals, with a street value at as much as $20,000! This was some serious stuff going on here and immediately I knew that tonight was going to be a fun night.

That night was the highest I'd ever been in my life. The great thing about meth was that along with the euphoric high, it gave me endless energy. Amanda and I stayed up for days from that night. Randall and Emilio began hanging out at our house all the time and I began to learn more about Emilio. He was a big time drug dealer, out of prison on parole, and back in business. In the meth world, most people sell drugs in grams, ounces or even quarter ounces. Emilio sold nothing less than pounds or kilos, in prices that started at $15,000.

This was new to me. I'd never been around anybody with that amount of drugs or that much money on them. I found Emilio exciting and interesting and a great resource for my addiction. Emilio's business drew even more people to Amanda's house and in no time, we became a popular drug stop. I was still dating Jackson, but Emilio was interested in me.

Emilio was sent back to prison for four months, and Jackson and I broke up. Amanda was so glad that I was done with Jackson. She and I had become a family, working together, making tons of money and doing a lot of drugs. I had grown so attached to her boys. Each night I'd give them their baths and read to them before bedtime. They'd ask to sleep with me at night and begged me to play games with them. In the morning, I was the one who got up at 5 a.m. to get myself ready and then wake the boys, get their breakfast and take them to day care. We played games in the car, and I came to love them and bond with them in a very special way. Looking back, it makes me sad to think that I did all of this through a haze of drugs. I loved those little guys.

Despite the love we shared in the family relationship, Amanda and I ended up getting into a big fight over drugs and she kicked me out.

I moved in with another friend named Jennifer, and her three-year-old son, Steele. Before long, our apartment was another kick-it spot for drug use, with Steele in the midst. I smoked meth, but Jennifer started shooting it, trying to get me to try it with her. I am deathly afraid of needles, so always declined and I took Steele into another room while Jennifer shot the deadly poison into her arm.

Jennifer eventually quit shooting meth after suffering from what we thought was a small stroke. She woke up one morning, unable to feel anything on the left side of her body. That was enough to get Jennifer to quit meth all together for a couple months.

But not me. I loved the lifestyle - partying, going to work high, and people over at our place all the time. I was living the good life, doing whatever I wanted, whenever I wanted. I was having fun all the time; getting high all the time.

I loved having the energy that meth gave me. Jennifer and I would stay up all night doing all kinds of crazy things. One of our favorite things to do would be go to a 24 hour Walmart and just browse for four or five hours in the middle of the night. I had forgotten all the morals my parents taught me as a child, and prided myself in how much Jennifer and I could shoplift as we walked around Walmart. We always bought a few items when we finally left the store, but it was common for us to steal hundreds of dollars worth of merchandise, just because we didn't have anything else to do in the middle of the night.

CHAPTER 6

LOSING IT ALL

*I*t seemed like my car was always in the repair shop. Once again it was inoperable and I had it towed to Amanda's house. But my car wasn't the only thing that was damaged. By now the meth had ravaged my body. The lack of sleep that meth induced had taken its toll on me. I was seriously underweight with big, dark circles under my eyes. My long naturally curly hair fell lifeless down my back and my complexion was sallow. The drugs ravaged my energy and I couldn't get up in the morning without reaching for the meth pipe.

Jennifer and I had been evicted from our apartment and we were living out of a storage unit or a KOA campground and sometimes with different friends. It was hard to dress for work living without a regular shower or closet. It was hard to look presentable for work with the meth draining so much from my body.

Somehow, I convinced my dad to loan me money to get my car fixed so I could keep my job. Despite my drug addiction, my job was my passion. I loved my job and I was good at it. I'd been promoted to brand manager and was responsible for all the store visuals and displays at Luxx. It was my dream job and I loved it. Amanda had quit as the manager and the new manager and I were really clicking. I was still working 70 hours a week and took a great deal of pride in my store.

About the only thing I liked better than my job was doing drugs. One night my friend Jacob decided that he wanted to make meth. Jennifer and I spent days cutting off the strike part of match books, and going from drug store to drug store, buying cold medicine all over town, purchasing as much as they would sell us.

Making meth was unlike anything I'd ever experienced before. Jacob began this home recipe for methamphetamines, mixing it all up in the bathtub. The fumes made me nauseous. My head began to hurt and I realized that Jennifer's little boy, Steele, was in the room watching all of this! I took Steele into the bedroom and put towels under the door and opened the window. "Come on," I said, "Let's read a story."

I called Jennifer into the bedroom where I had her son. "I'm going to pass out. We need to get out of here."

"Oh, it's not that bad," Jennifer said. "Let's just go to bed."

"But what about Steele?" I asked. "This isn't good for him to be around this stuff. And besides, Jacob is acting weird."

"I know, but I like him. We'll be all right," Jennifer said, not wanting to leave.

Amanda agreed to let me move back to her house. Since Amanda had quit her job, she and Randall were struggling and had no money. "Well, I'm working and making money," I told her. And so she and Randall welcomed me back to my old routine of looking after the kids and house, and this time I was buying the drugs. So I stayed back and forth with Amanda and Jennifer for awhile.

There had been another management shake up at Luxx and I had another new manager. I did my job well and things were going okay. The store looked beautiful and the district manager loved me and the way I set up the store displays and all the visuals. I think the attention and praise started to irritate the new store manager, and a bit of jealousy developed. One day, after sleeping late, I missed my shift. When I arrived at work late, my manager had my check ready. Despite the assistant manager's pleas to give me another chance, the manager terminated me. In a heartbeat, I lost the job I loved. I was devastated.

My life now was totally about drugs. Drugs were my daily emotion. Before I could even get out of bed in the morning, I would sit up and smoke meth to get high enough to start my day. I'd take a shower, smoke a little; start my make up, smoke a little more. Brush my teeth, smoke a little, dry my hair, smoke a little more. The meth gave me energy - so much so, that sometimes we would stay up for days, wandering department stores, driving around, cleaning house, scrapbooking, or even reading medical journals on drug addiction. The more meth I smoked, the less energy I seemed to gain from it, and unlike the early years of smoking meth, now I could sleep after using it. In the beginning I could stay awake for as many as 10 days without sleep; now I could only stay up for maybe three days at the most before I crashed.

My circle of drug friends was tightly knit. Within a drug family there are basic simple rules - you share and you keep quiet. That's just the way that it is. Everyone puts in some money to buy drugs for the day. It's called "smoking you out." It means that you share your money to get high. Whoever you're with is part of the group who shares with you. And you never talk about where the drugs came from with anyone.

When Amanda was working at Luxx, as a store manager, she would buy. When she quit and had no income, I bought. Now neither of us had a job, but we still had money for drugs. This was a tighter circle than a traditional family.

Emilio was released on parole. It took him about 30 seconds to open back up for drug business. I knew how much drug traffic was coming in and going out at Amanda's house. Emilio was a big distraction for Randall, and Amanda was getting scared at how involved Randall had drawn their family into Emilio's business. Frequently Emilio and Randall would be gone all night. Amanda would become so angry when Randall wouldn't answer his phone when he was off with Emilio and finally in her fury, she kicked Emilio out.

Emilio agreed to go, but since he didn't drive, he asked me to take him to a truck stop on Highway 99 where he could meet a friend. I dropped him off there and returned home to find Amanda and Randall and her boys at the house, just hanging out. I went over across the field, to Amanda's parents' house to use their computer. I wanted to search on-line for a new job.

I remember that I was sitting at their computer, googling around on a job search engine when I got a phone call from Emilio.

"Erin, why is Randall pulled over by an undercover cop?" Emilio asked me.

"How do you know that?" I asked. I'd just dropped Emilio off a few minutes ago. How could he know anything about where Randall was?

"Don't worry about it," Emilio assured me. "Just go over to the house and see if Randall's phone is there."

I stayed on the phone talking with Emilio as I ran over to the other house. I was shocked to see four strange cars all pulled up around our little farm house and when I got inside, there were all these unfamiliar people in the house wearing badges, but dressed in regular street clothes. I realized the cars had to be undercover police vehicles and these were cops raiding our place.

"Are you Erin?" a big, burly, bald guy asked me, with his gun drawn.

I looked at him, his gun, and the situation in the room and I spoke into the phone, "Um… I gotta go."

Emilio asked, "Are they there?"

"Yep," I sputtered and I closed my phone.

The big cop demanded, "Are you Emilio's girlfriend?"

"No!" I defended myself.

The cops were taking Randall outside.

"Where's Emilio?" the cop asked me.

My heart was beating a mile a minute. I swallowed. "I don't know," I told him.

"Sit down." The cop demanded and pointed to a chair. I walked toward the chair on wobbly legs, sat down and looked around surveying the situation. There were eight plain clothes cops, rummaging through all of our stuff. My heart leapt into my throat. I had meth in my purse, which was sitting on a dresser back in the boys' bedroom.

Damn! I had to get in to the boys' room, before the officers did. I didn't know how I was going to arrange that, but I didn't want them to find drugs in my purse.

The cop stood there, towering over me. "Do you have any identification?" he asked.

"Yes," I told him. "It's in my purse. Let me get it for you." I got up and he followed me into the boys' room. With my back to him, I fished in my purse for my wallet and snagged the small bag of meth. Before I turned around, I tucked the packet of drugs into my bra.

"Here." I said, turning and shoving my driver's license at him. "And I'm *not* Emilio's girlfriend."

He looked at my ID which had my mom's address on it. "How long have you lived at this address?" he asked, referring to Amanda's house. He escorted me outside on the front porch of the house, where I could see Randall.

Before I could answer that question, he fired another one at me. "When did you last talk to Emilio?" the cop asked, with an intimidating tone.

Amanda started screaming at me, "You tell them whatever they want to know, Erin!"

The cop leaned over and looked right into my face, "So are you going to tell me where he is?" he asked. His breath was hot and smelled like cigarettes.

"But I don't know where he is," I insisted.

"Don't you protect him!" Amanda screamed. "They're going to take my kids if you don't tell them. Just tell them what they want to know. Tell them! Erin! Tell them!" Amanda was totally panicked.

"But I don't know where he is," I told the cop. "I dropped him off at the Vallero truck stop on 99, but beyond that, I have no idea where he is, or who he's with."

"Listen," the cop was unrelenting. "We have all of you on drug charges, and aiding and abetting a convicted felon. Emilio's violated his parole, so whatever he's done with your help, we can book you on accessory charges. You're going to jail unless we find him."

By this time they had taken Randall back into the house, and the cops were searching everything. They had me sit on the porch steps. I knew they would find incriminating items that would surely send us to jail. The night before we'd smoked a little, and I knew they'd find our pipes and there was probably meth left over in those pipes. I knew at the very least they'd have us for would be possession.

The cop took command again, "We're going to arrest all of you," he explained. Amanda was freaking out, screaming about them taking her kids to Child Protective Services. I knew those boys were her world, and I loved them too. The whole situation was crazy, all to protect a convicted felon.

Dang! This was such a messed up situation for those little boys. The cops had brought Amanda outside with the boys. I was looking at them sitting on the ground with Amanda. The boys got up and began to climb in the trees in the yard. They were so innocent in all of this and unaware of most of what was happening. Those little boys deserved way better from the adults who loved them.

I sat there on the porch steps, and put my hands over my face. A younger white cop sat down next to me. "So," he said, with a less intimidating tone, "How long have you been doing meth?"

I looked up at him in disbelief. "Don't talk to me," I replied.

"You know, you should probably get some help," he persisted.

I put my head back into my hands. "Don't talk to me!" I demanded.

"That's not a very good attitude," he continued his one-sided conversation.

"Don't speak to me," I yelled at him. "I don't care who you are."

The big, bald cop was now interrogating Randall. When he finished he handcuffed Randall's hands behind his back and put him in the backseat of a big Dodge Durango SUV.

Next the big, bald cop came over to me on the porch, "Get in the car," he gestured toward the Durango.

"What?" I asked. "I'm not getting in the car."

"I'm taking you to jail, right now," he said. He pulled out another set of handcuffs, quickly cuffed me and put me in the backseat of that Durango with Randall.

I couldn't believe this! It was getting way too scary and real for me. I kept looking at Randall, and I asked, "What the hell is going on?"

Randall looked at me, even more bewildered. "I don't know. Erin, what do we do?"

"I don't know!" I cried, pulling on the handcuffs that were pinching my skin. "Why did they put us in this car? Where are we going?"

Randall sighed. "I'm going to take them to Emilio."

I gasped. Before I could say anymore, the bald cop opened the door to the car and removed the handcuffs from both Randall and me. With warning, he said, "I'm taking these off, but if you try anything, you're done."

"Okay," Randall said. "We'll wait." I just nodded.

Leaving Amanda and the boys behind, all eight cops got into the different vehicles parked in front of the house and we began a caravan to Modesto. Emilio knew a family in a farming community where he hung out regularly. An older couple and their son lived in a tiny house in rural Modesto and Emilio sometimes crashed with them. Randall told me that's where we were headed.

It took about a half hour for the undercover motorcade to get off the freeway and wind into a quiet rural area, with narrow farming roads and very few homes or farm buildings. Our caravan of cops drove by the tiny house to find no cars in the driveway, indicating no one was home. So the undercover agents drove past the house, into one of the orchards down the road. All of the cops got out of their vehicles and met in a small circle. Randall and I stayed in the Durango.

A female cop left the group, opened the door to the Durango and looked at me, "I thought you didn't know where he was?" she asked. She had my phone in her hand and was looking at my "Recent Calls" list.

"Your phone says you talked to Emilio at …." And she started reading all the times I'd spoken to Emilio that day. "Did you tell him we were there at the house? If you did, you're going to jail!" She slammed the car door and returned to the circle of agents.

I was beyond scared at this point. Randall and I were left sitting in the backseat of that Durango all afternoon, watching the cops plan what to do next. We sat there for several hours, until finally the sun began to set.

"I think this is a stakeout," I told Randall. It looked like a movie set, with the cars parked at angles and the cops all talking together. Randall and I could hear the cop radios squawk and radio broadcasts flash back and forth. "We're gonna move in at 2100 hours…"

Suddenly, the cops opened up the trunks and backs of the vehicles and began to strap on SWAT team gear. They put on Kevlar vests, then shirts that said "POLICE" on the back. Each of them began to strap on guns to their legs, ankles and tucking extra handcuffs into the back of their belts.

"Gosh! This is just like a movie," I exclaimed to Randall, baffled by the activity around us. The police began to arm themselves with shotguns, rifles with lasers and handguns. And then they began to wait, in anticipation of a shootout with Emilio. The whole time, Randall and I were just sitting in the backseat of that Durango.

A car drove by, and the police decided to move in. All four cars went swarming into the yard of the tiny house, lights flashing, sirens blaring. Randall and I were still in the backseat of that Durango; if there was any shooting, we were an easy target for crossfire. One of the police officers yelled through a megaphone, "Emilio Martinez! This is the police. Come out with your hands up!"

The cops were all strategically poised behind the car doors and around the house, with their firearms pointed, ready to fire at any activity.

But Emilio wasn't there.

The agents scoured that place, but they couldn't find a trace of Emilio. In an almost collective sigh of defeat, they began to wrap up the stake out and put all the gear back in their vehicles. Randall and I continued to sit in the backseat of the Durango wondering what was going to happen to us next.

Finally, when the last item was loaded back into the Durango, the cop started the SUV and we headed back to Amanda's farm house. On the way we stopped at a gas station. While they were re-fueling, another cop got into the Durango and handed me his business card. He had circled his cell phone number on it.

"Here's the deal," he said to me, and then looked at Randall. "If we can't find Emilio by tomorrow morning, you're both going to jail."

"What if you can't find him?" I asked. "I don't know where he is."

The cop looked grim. "We're taking you back to the house," he explained. "There will be a helicopter circling your house for the next 24 hours. During that time, neither of you can leave or invite anyone over."

"Okay," I said. "But what if you can't find him?"

"If anybody leaves or comes into that house," the cop ignored my question. "We're going to be there, like that!" And he snapped his fingers. "You're going on 'lock down' for the next 24 hours."

They brought us back home super late, and Amanda came out of the house, furious with me because I didn't disclose Emilio's location. "I will not let them take my kids away from me because you won't tell them where Emilio is!" she shouted.

I was exhausted, scared and didn't know what to expect. I went into the house and headed directly for my room. I sat down on my bed, wishing I had some meth to mellow my mood. With no drugs, I tried to unwind by playing solitaire and not thinking about the events from the past few hours. Then my phone chimed with a text message. It was from Emilio.

"Is everything cool?" it read.

"No," I sent a text back.

Then my phone rang and I could see that it was Emilio calling me. I didn't even say hello, I just picked up. "I don't want to talk to you, I don't want to know where you are," I said breathlessly. "It's crazy! The cops took us to Modesto looking for you. They probably have my phone tapped. So don't say a word. Don't tell me anything."

"All right," Emilio agreed, and the phone disconnected.

That night we heard the helicopter circling the farm where we lived. A search light would pour out occasionally, sweeping the pasture. Then next morning I told Randall about Emilio's text message and Randall called that number on the business card the cop had given us the night before.

I didn't want to call back, but Randall, like Amanda, was concerned about what would happen to their boys. Randall handed me the phone, "He did call last night, but I don't know where he is," I told him, "I don't know what to tell you."

We continued to be under surveillance for the next few days. Ultimately it was an ex-girlfriend of Emilio's who turned him in. Emilio was captured within a few days and returned to prison. Remarkably, none of us were arrested and Amanda and Randall were able to keep their little boys with them. It was enough of a scare that both Amanda and Randall made the decision to get "clean" and stop using drugs or hanging out with people who used drugs.

This decision had a big impact on my life. While I agreed that Amanda's boys deserved to live a better lifestyle, I could not give up my drug use. Amanda's message to me was, "You can stay here, but you can't do drugs in my house." She handed me a bag of meth. "I found this in kitchen," Amanda had tears in her eyes as she spoke. "Actually, Randall found it and gave it to me. At first we were going to throw it away," she continued. She looked down at the floor and then back at me. "But, we know how it is, so I'm going to give it to you. So here you go, here's the meth. Now you have to leave." I clutched the meth to my heart, hugged Amanda goodbye and said a tearful farewell to those two precious little boys that I loved so much.

CHAPTER 7

GET HIGH AND DIE

With no job, Emilio locked up, and no place to live, I started bouncing around from house to house for a few days. It didn't seem like my life could get much more stressful, until the transmission went out in my car. With no place to live and no money to pay for repairs I didn't know what to do. Amanda was willing to let me store the car at her house, so I had it towed back to the farm house.

Jennifer had moved into a small house on the outskirts of Stockton, with an older man. I moved in with them and Jennifer and I spent almost every minute together smoking meth. I started to realize that my life was a total mess. All I could think about now was getting high. My body and mind craved meth with an unbridled obsession that consumed every part of my body and soul. I didn't have anything else in my life. My parents and sister didn't want anything to do with me anymore; and I no longer had Amanda or her boys in my life, since I loved meth more than I loved them. I didn't have a job and even my treasured car was damaged with no hope of ever being able to get it fixed. Life just plain sucked and I wanted out.

On my 22nd birthday, Jennifer and I were at her friend Dylan's house, hanging out, getting high as hell. I looked at my life and I didn't like what I saw. I'd lost everything - my home, my family, my car and my job. I finally decided that I would just kill myself, and I'd do it by smoking myself to death.

I remember declaring to myself, "I'm going to smoke as much as I can. I'm just gonna finish it. This is my life. I've lost everything, so what's the point?"

Before these last few weeks, everything had been cool. I knew I was an addict, but I had been a *functioning* addict. Now I couldn't see any way out of this cycle. I was sucked into addiction and the only way out was to die. That appealed to me more than continuing to live as an addict.

By this time my weight had dropped to well below 100 pounds and normally, everyone in our group easily out-smoked me. I was always out early, compared to the rest of the party group. That night, however, I was determined to consume more than everyone else. I asked for more and more and my friends were accommodating.

I remember lying on Dylan's water bed, looking up at the ceiling, asking myself, "Why isn't this working?" I wanted to die so badly, and meth seemed like the best way to end my life. But no matter how much I smoked, I continued to breathe. Finally, I passed out. But the next morning I woke up. I was so angry. Damn! Why didn't it work? What was I going to do now?

So I got up and smoked some more – way more than I had ever smoked before, consciously knowing that this was a dangerous game I was playing, with dark, deadly consequences. I was determined to smoke myself to death with a meth overdose.

But even loading more and more methamphetamines into my body didn't kill me. I kept smoking, more and more meth, deeply inhaling noxious fumes that would have wiped out a person twice my size. Yet, I didn't die.

I found great frustration in that fact. I thought, "Dang! This totally sucks! I don't have the courage to slit my wrists or put a noose around my neck and hang myself. I'm even a failure at suicide! I just want to get high and die!"

When Dylan woke up, he told Jennifer and me that we had to leave. I didn't know what to do. I had no plan to go anywhere. I had nowhere to go. In all honesty, I hadn't planned on being alive on this day. Jennifer had no suggestions on where we could go either. I had no one and no place to live; everything had been lost because of my meth addiction. I had nothing I could count on in my life... except maybe my high school sweetheart, Brandon.

CHAPTER 8

ROCK BOTTOM

*M*y relationship with Brandon was always a possibility. In high school we had dated for two and a half years, but Brandon and I had continued to be in a relationship on and off since then for nearly six years. He had always been there for me. Brandon was the only friend I had who didn't use meth, and he had offered more than once to help me get clean. He was a rock of support and had sent me money when I needed it, offered me safe refuge when I had nowhere else to go, and had always granted help every time I'd asked in the past.

So, abandoning my dignity, I called Brandon.

"Erin! What's going on with you?" Brandon asked when he picked up the phone.

"I need your help," I told him. "I need you to come and get me. Right now."

Without hesitation Brandon answered, "I'll be right there."

The meth had ravaged my body and when Brandon came to get me, he didn't find the stylish, bouncy, vivacious girl he'd known in high school. Instead he found a frail, malnourished, darkly depressed meth addict, with wild hair, ashen complexion and empty soul.

Brandon had no tolerance for people using meth. He took one look at me and said, "Erin, you have to get off drugs."

I nodded and picked up my bag. Brandon helped me get into the car.

"I think you should see a doctor," Brandon said before he even started the ignition. "Let me help you get into a rehab program."

I started to cry, "No, I don't want to go to rehab."

"You can't keep on using, Erin," Brandon looked at me from the driver's seat. "I'm scared for you. I'll pay for rehab, Erin. Please?"

"I just need to sleep," I said to Brandon. My body was so sore, I just wanted to rest.

"All right," Brandon agreed. He started the car and took me back to his place in Manteca, a small community south of Stockton.

For the next few days, I just rested at Brandon's house. I couldn't get out of bed. Brandon brought meals to me in bed. I'd eat a bit, but I was so weak, even snacking would sap my energy. I hurt all over, and even breathing was painful. After just a few sips of soup, I would fall back to sleep as my body recovered from my attempt at suicide. Each time Brandon would talk to me, he insisted that I needed to get into a rehabilitation program. I always thanked him, but declined.

On the sixth day at Brandon's house, I was beginning to feel a little bit better. Brandon tried one more time. "Erin, you have to get some help," he insisted. "You need to go to rehab."

"I'm getting better," I replied. "I don't want to go to rehab. I'll be okay. I'm getting stronger, and I'll be fine."

"Look, I've found a place that you can go for treatment," Brandon said kindly. "I'll pay for it. It's a nice place where you can rest and recover. This is a disease Erin, and you need treatment for it."

"I can do this on my own," I told him. "I don't need to be locked up in a hospital. I'll be fine."

Brandon was unrelenting. "No, you won't be fine. You have to get some help."

I continued to argue, "No, I'll get clean. I promise. But I'll do it my way."

Brandon shook his head sadly. "Sorry Erin," he said getting up from the edge of the bed. "But if you aren't going into rehab, then you can't stay here." He left the bedroom, softly closing the door behind him.

"Fine!" I yelled at the door. "I don't need you!" And I started to cry, feeling a terrifying wave of desperation wash over me once again. Without Brandon, I had no one.

CHAPTER 9

I HAVE A PROBLEM

---

*B*randon was serious about no longer helping me if I wasn't willing to enter a formal rehabilitation program. He gave me a couple days to figure out what I was going to do and where I was going to go, but he made it clear that I couldn't stay with him any longer. I felt so alone, abandoned and without hope. I had been a strong, independent woman with direction, goals and a life plan. Now I was weak, needy and without hope.

With grave anxiety I placed the toughest phone call I've ever made in my life. I called my mom.

"Mom," I breathed into the phone. "I have a problem."

"I think you're right," Mom surprised me with her answer. "How can I help?"

"I don't know what I'm going to do," I told her. "My life is so messed up. I've lost everything. Jennifer and I got kicked out of our house, I lost my job and the transmission went out in my car. I don't know what to do."

My mom was quiet for a minute. Then she said, "Well, I might be able to help get your transmission fixed. I could do that for your birthday present."

"Oh, that would be great," I sighed. "I'm at Brandon's house. If you can come to Manteca tomorrow, that would be so cool."

Mom had moved to Sacramento and was now living about an hour north of me. She didn't answer me about that proposal right away. I held my breath, expecting her to tell me no. It wasn't a quick trip down the freeway to find me now, and maybe she wouldn't come after all. I waited, expecting the worst, as she said, "Erin, I have resources that can help you."

I was still pretty shaky, but I persisted, "I don't know what to do. Brandon says I can't stay here," I replied. "If we can get my car running again, that would be a big help."

"Well, my resources might be able to help with more than your car," Mom answered.

"I just need my car fixed," I told her again.

Mom kept referring to her "resources." I kept thinking, "What the hell are you talking about it? Just fix my car!" but I didn't say that to her, because I needed her help.

Mom offered to pick me up the next day. Brandon woke me up the next morning and I tried to drag myself into alertness. I took one look in the mirror and groaned. "I can't let her see me like this!" I whispered.

I was a mess. Dragging myself into the shower was painful and trying to dry my hair took every ounce of strength I had. By the time I finished a simple task of combing my hair, I had barely enough strength to dust some powder over my face. I sat in front of the mirror shocked at what I saw. The girl in the mirror couldn't be me! This girl in my mirror was a skeleton with gray skin and scary dark circles under her eyes. Her hair was flat and lifeless and there was no sparkle in her red-rimmed eyes. This could not be the girl my mother was coming to help.

Erin's mom, Lisa remembers it this way

Lisa -

After my divorce from Erin's father, I moved to Sacramento, where I began a relationship with Dillon, a wonderful Christian man. He led me to the Lord and to a Christian church that taught me to put my trust in God and to build all relationships on a foundation of God's love.

I had told Dillon all about Erin's trials and that I was honestly afraid that I was going to lose her. I thought that sooner or later, Erin would die from drug addiction. Dillon assured me that God was going to save my daughter. He said it with such conviction that I was inspired. Erin had led our family through scores of crisis and I had given up on her. I wanted to trust in the power of God, but I had my doubts. I didn't have that level of trust in Him yet and I wanted desperately to believe Dillon's promise.

When Erin called, I knew she was in trouble. The tremble in her voice and the desperation in her tone made her sound like a frightened little girl, hopeless and lost. It broke my heart, but I braced myself to employ the tough love I'd learned to use in the past few years. Erin had told so many lies and manipulated her dad and me so many times that I was prepared to be stoic to whatever her current crisis was. I had learned not to be emotionally invested in her drug-related issues anymore. I was done with all of it. But it still hurt me to see my child in pain.

I could tell from our brief telephone conversation that Erin was as low as I'd ever known her to be before. As she explained that she'd lost her home, job, friends and her car, I sensed that Erin felt she had nothing left to lose by calling me.

I didn't want to bring Erin back into my life. I was afraid of being hurt all over again and of living with someone that I couldn't trust. All of us in Erin's family had tried repeatedly to help her, but every time she would recoil in defiance and return to her drug culture and the friends who supported her in pursuit of another high. Drugs were always more important than anything to Erin.

I agreed to drive to Manteca, where Brandon lived, the next day to see about getting Erin's car fixed. She didn't ask if she could come home again, and I didn't offer. "One step at a time," I thought and I began to pray for courage and wisdom to guide my daughter back to sobriety.

I woke up the next morning more doubtful than ever that I could do what I felt God calling me to do. I opened my Bible and read my morning scriptures, hesitant to get going.

Trust in the Lord with all your heart and lean not on your own understanding.

Proverbs 3:5

"Father God," I prayed. "I don't think I can do this. I'm so afraid of what I'll find when I get to Erin and I'm so afraid that anything I do will be the wrong thing. I just want to help my little girl, but I've tried and failed so many times, I really don't know how to help. Please, please, guide me."

The tears were pouring down my face and I felt God tugging at my heart to trust Him. I read the words in Proverbs again in my Bible and prayed again, "I can't do this Lord. I don't want to do this, Father!" It was one thing to profess to trust God in all things; it was another to actually be willing to act on that trust. I did not want to go through another war with my daughter.

Yet, I felt God gently nudging me, quietly encouraging me to go to my daughter. I re-read my scripture again, trying to glean whatever message might be there. I could feel my stress level go up as I struggled with where God was leading me.

Again I prayed, "I want to follow your direction, Father, but I don't think I have the strength to do it. Please give me insight to do whatever you want me to do." I felt like I was in a battle with God, with him telling me to go and me arguing with him. God was so patient with me that morning, softly whispering encouragement into my heart as I cried and prayed.

Finally, I took a deep breath, as a divine peace came over me. "Okay, I guess I'll go," I conceded to God. "But you're going with me!"

I touched up my makeup, grabbed my purse and car keys, and got into my car to head south. It was a foggy, dismal morning as I got on the Hwy 99 freeway. I put an upbeat, contemporary praise CD in the car's sound system and continued my conversation with God as I prepared a plan to help my little girl. As I drove, I kept talking with God as I sang along with the CD.

Strength will rise, as we wait upon the Lord
We will wait upon the Lord
We will wait upon the Lord
Our God, You reign forever
Our hope, our Strong Deliverer
You are the everlasting God

As the music filled my car, that holy peace swirled around me and I found myself trading trepidation for courage. Whatever I found when I got to Erin, I could face with God as my co-pilot. "You're the defender of the weak, you comfort those in need, you lift us up on wings like eagles," *I sang more of the words to the song. I could do this, with God's help. Erin was my daughter, my first-born child, and no matter what she had done, I loved her with all my heart. She would always be my little girl – my gift from God. I had a fresh and new resolve – I was sustained by my faith and my trust in God.*

I pulled up to Brandon's apartment complex to find Erin sitting on the stairs. She looked terrible; nothing like the bright- spirited character that used to fill our house with merriment. This hollowed-out young woman was dangerously thin, pale and a mess. She saw my car and pulled herself to her feet and began to descend the stairs. The closer Erin got, the more little and broken she looked.

I had flashbacks to Erin's earlier years of high fashion and style when she wouldn't even go out to get the newspaper if she wasn't fixed up. I grieved for the spark and fire that used to radiate from her laughter. Meth had robbed my daughter of her inner and outer beauty and she was barely a shell of what God had created her to be. I held my breath as she approached, and I feared that I was not prepared for the next step, whatever that was.

Erin made it to the car, and carefully got in and closed the door. "Hi," *she said. She just sort of sat there as I absorbed all that I observed. I smiled sadly and then she started to cry.*

I gave her a hug. I had decided that I couldn't cry. So I resisted the urge to wrap myself in her grief and instead held her for a moment, stroking her hair. "It's okay. I'm here now. We'll figure it out."

My intent was to just spend the day with Erin and bring her back to Brandon's after arranging to get her car fixed. I had the car towed to a transmission repair place and then we went to lunch while they accessed the car repairs.

After lunch Erin and I went to Target. Before we got out of the car Erin looked at me and said, "Brandon says I have to be gone by the end of the week."

We went into the store and I grabbed a shopping cart, heading toward the house wares department, while Erin went in another direction. I called Dillon, looking for advice.

"I don't know what to do!" I said in frustration. "She looks so little and fragile. I'm afraid I'll lose her permanently if I don't help her. But I'm afraid to bring her home and start that cycle all over again. What do I do?"

Dillon was calm and confirmed the peace I had felt earlier. "I'm sure you'll do the right thing, Lisa. We've been praying for Erin for months. God loves her too. If you're listening to the Lord, He will lead you to the right decision. You will figure this out. Call me on your way home." I hoped he was right as I hung up the phone and breathed a sigh and a prayer for guidance and direction.

The day went on and Erin and I had a pretty nice day. I resisted the urge to hand out unsolicited wisdom all day. I offered no lectures, no sermons, and no recriminations. It appeared that Erin really did want to make changes in her life. This day she seemed open to anything. She was so frail and shaken that I think she wasn't really able to make a decision or even think. She was submitting to me to help her and to bring her to the resources I had told her about.

The Lord warmed my heart with Erin's state of mind and before I knew it, I asked her, "Would you like to spend the night at my house? I can make dinner and you can sleep in Erica's room." As I said this, I could hardly believe those words popped out of my mouth. But I remembered the words from Proverbs that morning, "Trust in the Lord with all your heart and lean not on your own understanding." I didn't understand, but I was trusting my God.

I could see relief wash over Erin. "Yes. That would be nice. I would like to come home with you," she said softly.

My Dad and I on my Grandparents boat

My mom and I at my Grandparents house 9 months

My 1ˢᵗ birthday

Waterski trip in motor home1991

Erica and I, Stockton 1991

Easter, 1992

Tubing on the Delta with Jerry, Rob and Glen 1995

On the delta 1996

Dad and I 8th grade graduation

Christmas 1999 with cousins Andy and Teddy

Winter formal freshman year, 2000

4th of July delta vacation 2002

High School Graduation Picture 2004

High school graduation 2004

Elizabeth and I 2009

Erica's rehearsal dinner May 2010

Erica's Wedding May 2010

Mom, Erica and I, Erica's wedding May 2010

Erica's wedding; Andy, Mom, Erica, Spencer, Me, Tina

Labor Day on Folsom Lake 2010

Danelle and I South Beach, Miami September 2010

Danelle and I Bahamas Cruise September 2010

California Marathon 2010

CHAPTER 10

HOME SWEET HOME

*M*om drove me to her new house in Sacramento and she showed me to my sister Erica's room. Erica was living away at college, and her empty room looked like heaven to me. I took a shower while Mom fixed me something to eat. I nibbled on her home cooked meal and then I got into bed. That bed was so soft, I felt like I was sleeping on a cloud. The down comforter that I pulled up around me was soft and snuggly and I drifted off to sleep, feeling more safe and secure than I had in a long, long time. My body ached with the withdrawal pain of methamphetamines.

Erin's mother Lisa recalls this week

I hadn't intended to bring Erin home. I just wanted to get her car fixed and be done with her problems. I was a relatively new in my Christian walk and I had just begun to be a regular worshiper at Bayside Church. I didn't have a long history with trusting God. I clung to the promises I had learned and looked to Bayside Church for guidance. As soon as we got home, I called the Community Care Center at Bayside for help. I left a message, but no one called me back.

I attended a weekly Tuesday night Bible study, and I invited Erin to go with me. I was stunned when she agreed. I'd confided in my study group about Erin's addiction at previous meetings, and they had been praying for her. That night, I was overwhelmed as the women in the group welcomed Erin with sincere warmth and friendship. We were doing a Beth Moore study, titled "Breaking Free" which included a video and then discussion afterward. I was encouraged by how Erin interacted with the other women and seemed to be interested in the topic. Breaking free was exactly what my prayer was for Erin. The other women in the group had been praying for Erin for weeks for the same thing. That night, all of us in our group laid hands on Erin and prayed for her together.

The next day Erin slept the entire day, getting up just to shower, eat a small lunch and go back to bed. Her fragile state worried me, and I felt so sad to see the spark gone from my daughter who once bounced around our house, laughing and dancing about the smallest victories in her life. With no return call from Community Care Center, I called the Bayside Church Women's Ministry leader, to find out that she was currently unavailable. I was assured that I would hear from her soon. But by the end of the day, I hadn't heard back from her or from anyone in the Community Care Center. Erin continued to sleep and I continued to pray. It was strange having her there. She was so quiet and demanded nothing from me.

Undaunted with the lack of response from my Bayside leaders, I continued to pray. I looked on the church website and found the contact information for a program called "Celebrate Recovery." I called Jeff Redmond, the director of the program, who picked up on the first ring. I briefly outlined Erin's history and the current situation. "Erin's here with me, now," I told Jeff. "But I don't know what to do. Can you meet with us? I am not equipped to handle this."

"Would you like me to meet with you today?" Jeff asked.

"Yes, please," I said breathlessly. I called to Erin, to ask how long it would take her to get ready and relayed the information to Jeff.

"I'll see you and Erin at Bayside in an hour," Jeff said. Finally! I had a Christian resource for my daughter.

When Mom asked me to get up and get dressed to go to Bayside with her, I had no idea where we were going or why. The women at Mom's Bible study were very nice and I found their study interesting, but I was a confirmed atheist and I did not believe there even was a God. But Mom was being pretty good to me, so what could this hurt?

We got to her church, which didn't look like a church at all. Bayside Church looked like a sprawling modern college campus, with two story buildings sprinkled around about 40 acres of landscape. Jeff met us in the lobby of the worship center. Instantly I knew that this guy was not a typical minister. Right off Jeff told me he was a recovered addict and in two seconds I could tell that he knew how to talk to me.

Jeff asked me questions about my life that made me realize that he had been where I was. I told him honestly about all the conflict and complications drug use had created for me. I felt like I could talk to him openly. To me, Jeff wasn't a pastor; Jeff was a guy who'd been in those same deep dark places I'd been. His counsel seemed to mean more coming from someone who had lived my life in the drug world. He wasn't a perfect pastor, living a perfect life; he was a real guy who had lived with the same addiction I did. Jeff also represented the first person outside of my family who seemed to care about me.

"I can't do this anymore," I told him. "Meth has stripped me of everything I love."

Jeff was empathetic, but not sympathetic. He offered himself as evidence that an addict could get clean and remain clean.

I wasn't convinced. I told him, "I tried to kill myself last week."

He didn't flinch when I continued. "It didn't work. I'm mad as hell. I can't even kill myself! I need help!" I railed.

Jeff asked me, "Erin, what kind of help do you think you need?"

"I don't know," I told him, sniffling. "But I know I need something."

Jeff nodded, "That's a good attitude to start with. Through Celebrate Recovery we have several treatment options. Do you want to check into an in-patient program?"

"I don't know," I told him.

"There's a program called Teen Challenge, that's very successful," Jeff said. "It's a year-long in-patient program that helps you rebuild your life."

"No way!" I told him. "I'm not committing to living some place for a whole year! That's not happening."

Jeff didn't react with alarm to my reply. "You don't have to decide right now. Go home and think about it."

"I just want to get help," I said.

Jeff smiled. "Maybe God has a plan for your life," he suggested.

"I don't really care about my life right now," I replied.

Jeff put his hands on my face, and then softly he said, "But God does. Erin, God loves you."

I didn't know what to make of this. I was a hard core atheist. I thought that anyone who believed in God was freakin' nuts! And now I had this guy talking to me about God like God was in the room with us.

"All right," I said, placating Jeff. "What does that mean? Why would God even care about me? I'm not worth much. My life is a mess."

Jeff smiled, and with a twinkle in his eye replied. "Erin, you're worth it. God loves you and has a plan for your life."

Then he quoted a Bible verse. It was Jeremiah 29:11 "For I know the plans I have for you," declares the Lord, "plans to prosper you and not to harm you, plans to give you hope and a future."

"Trust me," Jeff said looking me straight in the eye. "God has a plan for you."

I looked at him doubtfully. What the heck was he talking about? How could God know me, and even if he did, why would God think I was worth anything after all the things I'd done over the past few years?

Jeff invited me to a college group that night at the church. It was called The Shore, and it met right there in that same building. "There will be a whole bunch of college kids here. There's usually a message, some great music and it's really fun. Why don't you come?" He was so encouraging and it seemed important to him that I attend. "And you might also want to attend Celebrate Recovery, which meets tomorrow night."

My mom was sitting there and I saw her nodding at me. "All right I'll think about it. Maybe I'll check it out," I told him.

Jeff prayed with me, and it seemed like he was really talking to a person when he prayed. I don't really remember what he asked God for, but I felt Jeff's concern for me was genuine and I wasn't uncomfortable with his prayer.

"I know that your next days are going to be rough," Jeff said. "In fact, your next few months are going to be rough. Here's my card. If you're feeling weak, if you feel like you're going to start using again, just call me. I'll help you. And God will help you, Erin."

I thought he was crazy, but he got me thinking.

CHAPTER 11

THINKING

*M*om took me home. I felt a little bit different, but nothing dramatic. I kept thinking, "Wow, I don't even know this guy but he cares so much about me."

Jeff was inspiring because he repeatedly told me that he had been where I was. Jeff had walked in the darkness of alcohol addiction and understood the same pain and loneliness that I was experiencing. When Jeff said, "I know how you feel," I believed that he really did know how I was feeling. This was very encouraging and helped me open my mind to the possibilities about God that he described.

I was still exhausted as I crashed from the meth withdrawal. I slept awhile and early that evening my mom checked in on me.

"Do you want to go?" she asked me, referring to The Shore, Bayside's college group meeting. I could tell she was hopeful that I would go, but she wasn't pushing me.

"Yeah," I said. "I'll go check it out."

Since my car was still in the shop, Mom had to drive me to the church. I felt like I was 13 again, with my mother-chauffeur. Mom dropped me off in the Bayside parking lot at 7:30 and I waved good bye as she drove away.

I took a deep breath and walked on to the campus, toward the church sanctuary. Inside I found the room humming with cheerful chatter, and several tables set up in the entryway. There was a guest table for people who were new and other tables where people were sitting around and talking together.

People, all college age, just started coming up to me. "Hi what's your name?" Several strangers asked, extending a handshake in friendship and welcoming me to the event.

I didn't know what to make of their interest. I remember thinking, "Oh this is weird; these people are interested in me. I wonder why."

I located Raelynn, the girl Jeff had told me to look for. She gave me a little bag of welcome items, and then took me around the church, introducing me to all sorts of friendly people. Since Raelynn was in the worship team and would be on stage for most of the service, she found someone for me to sit with. I sat down a few minutes before the service started. I noticed that on stage there were several guitars lined up and a drum set. This wasn't what I expected.

The band started playing a rock and roll style praise song, loud and full of bass and I thought, "All right! This is new. This is different. It doesn't seem like church at all."

I looked around and everyone was really in a good mood, singing to the songs. I didn't really know what to do, but I looked around and tried to pick up on some of the words to the songs, which were being shown in a slide show on giant super-sized TV screens. People were raising their hands in the air, celebrating.

"This is different," I thought to myself.

After the band played awhile more, they stopped and a guy named John Harris came on the stage to talk and everyone sat down. He started talking and within about two minutes, I figured out that everything he was saying was a message that fit me to a T. I was astounded at how the message was exactly applicable to my life. I perked up and really started listening. I was focused on the message and fascinated at how this guy on a stage could know so much about what I needed in my life.

He finished up his message with words about God's love. John explained that Jesus was the son of God and would enter my heart if I wanted him to. He asked us if we wanted Jesus to be our personal savior.

I thought, "Maybe I do. I could use this right about now."

John instructed the entire assembly to close their eyes and invited us to pray with him. He said, "Jesus, I know I need you in my life, and I invite you into my heart to be my Lord."

Then John spoke to all of us, and said, "Nobody is looking around. Everyone's eyes are still closed. If you prayed that prayer tonight with me, just raise your hand, so I can pray for you this week. Don't by shy, I won't embarrass you in any way, just raise your hand and I'll pray for you this week."

Timidly, I barely raised my hand. The service ended and as I walked out of the church, everyone continued to be really friendly. I said my goodbyes and headed to the parking lot where Mom was waiting. I got in the car and Mom asked, "Well, how was it?"

I looked at her in wonder. "Oh my God, it was so cool!" I exclaimed. "I've never been to anything like that in my life. They were nice to me. Really, really nice to me!"

Mom was grinning, "Do you think you want to go back?" she asked carefully.

"I can't wait to go back next week!" I exclaimed. "I can't believe how cool it was!" I felt a tiny nudge of awakening in my soul.

CHAPTER 12

A NEW HOME – A NEW LIFE

hen Mom picked me up from Brandon's house, it was with the understanding that it was just until my car was repaired. The day after my first visit to The Shore, we drove down to get the car. We hadn't discussed where I was going, or where I would live. We just focused on the car. Mom paid a hefty $5000 repair bill, and then she drove me out to Amanda's house where I picked up five black garbage bags filled with my clothes and personal items.

From there Mom helped me secure car insurance and pay off all my outstanding tickets from Pasadena so that I could re-register my car. By the end of the day, Mom had paid more in repair, fines and fees than what my car was worth. I knew she wasn't happy about it, but unlike previous encounters like this, she didn't complain or lecture me. Since I still didn't have current California vehicle license tags, Mom promised to closely follow me back to her house, to avoid a CHP officer noticing my out of date license plates.

I was elated. Mom was willing to let me stay with her for a few more days. I was beginning to believe that maybe I could clean up my life, especially if all that stuff I'd heard at Bayside was really true. When we pulled into the driveway, I unloaded the sad remains of my life in those black garbage bags, and dragged them into the garage.

"I'm serious this time, Mom," I told her. "I want you to help me clean out my car and together we're going to get rid of anything that could possibly link me back to meth."

First, we took the car apart, pulling up the carpeting, taking the seats out and carefully examining all the places where I might have stashed meth or drug paraphernalia. The car was my sanctuary more than once and I was feeling such a craving for drugs that I knew if I found anything I would use it without even considering the consequences.

Next, we started going through the garbage bags, stuffed with expensive clothing that I had from my job at Luxx. Mom helped me sort it all, and it was humiliating to have all that I owned dumped on the floor of the garage. I gave Mom strict instructions, "Go through everything. Look in every pocket, every place where I might have stashed something."

"Are you sure?" Mom asked. I could tell she was eager to get started, but trying to respect my privacy as well. "You want my help?"

"I mean it, Mom." I nodded and started turning the pockets inside out on the jeans I was holding, "I am so weak, I can't have anything to tempt me. I need your help."

We worked together, quietly, sorting the clothes for laundering after we searched each item. We found little used foil packets, and other pieces of my drug life. Mom didn't react, she just helped me throw it all away, and I stopped apologizing. It was what it was.

Then I remembered that I had a pipe in my purse.

"Mom, find a sock for me," I demanded. "I'm going to show you just how serious I am about getting off meth. Wait here, I'll be right back." I ran into the house, down the hall to my room and found the glass pipe I used to smoke meth hidden in my purse. I grabbed it and ran back out to the garage. Mom was standing there looking at me curiously, holding a pink fuzzy sock. "Thanks!" I grabbed the sock and dramatically held up the pipe, "I knew I had this, but you didn't. I'm telling you that I have it because I want to show you just how serious I am about quitting." I snatched the sock from Mom, and then slipped the pipe into the pink sock. Then I put the sock on the floor and stomped on it with my boot. We could both hear the crunch of the glass as I crushed the pipe.

I looked at my mom and with determination I said, "I'm serious, Mom. I'm really, really serious." I picked up the glass-filled sock and threw it in the garbage can.

Mom and I kept sorting through the clothes and other items in the garbage bags, and we continued to clean the car. She began to ask me about meth and the deadly grip it had on me. Slowly I could feel us beginning to bond again. We were once so close and we used to have so much fun together.

"How do you use it?" Mom asked. She didn't have to elaborate. I knew what she meant.

"I smoke it," I told her.

"What does it look like?" Mom asked.

"It's like white shards of glass," I told her candidly.

"What does it smell like when you light it?" Mom asked.

"Like burning paint," I admitted. "Sometimes you put it on foil, and heat it up. Then you smoke the fumes."

Mom wrinkled her nose. "What does it feel like?"

I was craving meth; coming down now for my fifth day and my body ached all over. All I could think of was the great euphoria that I associated with the magic meth. "It's like, ahhhhhh." I sighed.

Mom continued to ask questions about the drug culture and my former lifestyle and I kept answering her honestly. We finished cleaning the car and sorted all my clothes and I was exhausted. I went to my room to sleep.

Mom woke me in time for a small dinner and then she drove me to Bayside Church for the Celebrate Recovery night. Jeff Redmond was there, and he introduced me to Catherine, who was warm and welcoming. "Hi, I'm so glad you're here," she said, extending her hand in greeting. "I've been clean for a year and a half now. And I'd love to be your accountability partner." She introduced me to a few other girls, and they gave me their phone numbers as well. We went on to a small group of other women who were also working on recovering from substance abuse. Together we all walked into the church.

It started much like The Shore college night the night before, with a great band playing loud contemporary music and then a pastor's message. After that, Catherine led me into a women's group where they started to go around the room to share their thoughts or experiences. I looked around the room and noted that there were about 25 women in this drug and alcohol abuse group. I was willing to sit there and listen, but I thought to myself, "I'm not talking in front of all these people!"

Each person was given about three minutes to speak to the group. My heart started beating and I was so nervous. I did not want to talk, especially to all these strangers about the topic they were talking about. Eventually it was my turn. I looked at Catherine and she nodded encouragement to me. I gulped, "This is my first time here. I've been clean for a couple days," I stammered. "I don't want to talk about it."

I went home that night wondering what I had gotten myself into. I wanted what they offered at Bayside, but in the next few weeks, as I suffered from meth withdrawal, I knew that I couldn't do this. I couldn't stay away from drugs forever. It was just a matter of time before I caved and went back to the seductive pull of meth.

I craved meth with every pore of my body. I was so tired that I could barely get out of bed in the morning just to take a shower, and once I did shower, I had to go back to bed to sleep before I could even dry my hair or put on my make up. As the drug slowly left my body, I suffered from all the typical withdrawal symptoms. I was panicked that I would return to my friends who I knew would give me drugs. With the panic, I also felt as if there were bugs inside my skin, crawling inside me and I was helpless to get them out.

More than once I called Mom and said, "I can't do this. I'm in so much pain. I know I'm going to use. I know I'm going to be back on drugs, no matter what I do."

Mom would come home from her job and I felt so bad that she was missing work, but so grateful that she would come home to help me. I kept going to The Shore on Thursday nights and Celebrate Recovery on Friday nights. Mom took me to church on Sunday mornings and to her Bible study on Tuesday nights. I was immersed in Bayside ministries and being held up in prayer by countless people I didn't even know. But the meth's sinister pull was always gripping every part of me and it wouldn't let go. Many times

I called Jeff or Catherine or Mom begging for their assurance that I could beat meth and leave that lifestyle behind me. I was never confident that they were right.

Mom was so good to me, but I knew she was worried. I was worried. I feared that I would start using again every day. I couldn't let go of my past and I missed the comfort of my drug using friends. In desperation, I called Emilio.

When my mom found out that I'd called Emilio it was the first time I felt that old familiar disapproval of the old days when I was proud to be a meth user. I wanted to visit Emilio and Mom was bold in her answer. "No, you're not!"

I understood her position and conceded that she was right. But then, Mom stepped over the line. She called Brandon and told him that I had called Emilio. That ignited an anger I hadn't felt in a long while, and I was ready to pack up and move out. With only a few days clean, I was still in pain from withdrawal and desperate to satisfy my addiction to meth. I thought I was managing that balance with Mom's support, but when she violated my confidence by talking to Brandon, it rocked my world. Even though I had nowhere else to go, I just wanted out of her house.

CHAPTER 13

RULES

---

*M*om knew she'd made a mistake and begged me not to go.

"Erin," Mom said through her tears. "I'm so sorry. I didn't know who to talk to about this, and I didn't think about your feelings. Please forgive me."

I was still angry and ready to get in the car and just drive away. Even though I didn't want to return to a drug lifestyle, I was ready to head that direction, just to escape the humiliation and hurt.

"Let's make an appointment with Jeff," Mom said. "He knows how you feel and maybe he can help me help you."

"I'm just getting out of here!" I said, stuffing my meager belongings into a bag. "I can't stay here if you don't respect me."

"Erin," Mom cried. "Please. I don't want you to go. Please, let's find a way to work through this. Please. I don't want you to go."

I turned around and looked at my mom. She looked so sad. "Okay." I said.

Mom and I met with Jeff Redmond the next day. As busy as he was, Jeff always seemed to be able to just clear his calendar for me. Together we sat down in his office and again, I felt Jeff's empathy.

"So, how are you doing?" he asked. "How many days clean are you now?"

That was Jeff's style. No dancing around the topic; he knew what I was and yet he accepted me just as I was. No judgment, just concern.

"I'm moving out," I stated flatly. "I can't do this."

"Sure, you can," Jeff said casually.

Mom and I each told our side of the story while Jeff listened. And then he helped us define an adult mother-daughter relationship.

"Erin," he took me by the hand, "This is your mother and she is your last hope. You have to respect her. She deserves your respect."

I nodded, and sighed. "I know. But she's so controlling. She can't stay out of my business!"

"But can you take care of your own business right now?" Jeff asked kindly, but he didn't wait for an answer. Instead, to my surprise, he turned to my mom.

"Lisa," Jeff said. "Erin is your daughter, but she's not a little girl. She's 22 years old. She's an adult. Can you accept that?"

Mom nodded and took my other hand. "Yes, but it's hard to know how to support her in recovery, if I don't help her make decisions."

Jeff looked at both of us, "Erin, you need to stay with your mom through recovery. You need her love and support to remain clean. Do you agree?"

I nodded, knowing he was exactly right. "And Lisa," Jeff continued. "If you want to live in harmony, then you will have to learn not to be controlling; to respect Erin as an adult, and to support her in her recovery and living in sobriety. Can you do that?"

I looked at my mom, who was nodding her head through her tears. She clutched my hand harder and I squeezed it back. I knew in my heart that she was my last hope, and I didn't want to leave.

"Okay, we are all in agreement that you can live in an adult mother-daughter relationship," Jeff said. "I want the two of you to sit down and draft some rules that both of you agree on."

"What kind of rules?" I asked.

"Rules about you living with your mother," Jeff said. "Rules about how to support you in sobriety that still allow you some privacy and dignity."

So that night, I sat at the kitchen table, while Mom fixed dinner, and together we agreed upon the following rules:

Mom's Home

1. *Be 100% honest with each other.*
2. *Erin is allowed to make her own decisions… mom is entitled to voice an opinion or suggestions. Erin must have an open mind about what mom has to say.*
3. *Respect each other.*
4. *Erin is not under any circumstances allowed any guests or visitors 3450 Westeria Lane without mom's permission.*
5. *Mom is allowed at any time to search any of Erin's belongings.*
6. *I Erin Kalte consent to take a drug test at any point in time when asked by Lisa Kalte.*
7. *When a challenge/issue arises we will sit down and talk about it… i.e. NO YELLING.*
8. *If Erin brings any type of drugs in or around 3450 Westeria Lane, Erin is gone. Not welcome back.*
9. *Erin is allowed to associate with whoever she wants.*
10. *Erin must ask/inform Mom when leaving the house. i.e. where she is going.*
11. *Mom allows Erin to choose her friends, DON'T PUSH!*

When we were finished, I made a copy of the rules and each of us posted them in our respective bedrooms. Once the rules were defined, Mom and I had no more conflicts.

CHAPTER 14

THE PAIN OF RECOVERY

*T*he first two weeks of being off meth, I didn't even get out of bed. By the third week, I was able to get up for a couple hours, but then I'd be back to bed, not even able to get dressed. I'd been on meth for so long and so consistently, coming down but then bouncing back on it, my body was unaccustomed to being clean.

Staying with Mom was a "home detox" facility. But unlike medical detoxification treatment, I had no medication for pain, or other physiological issues. I didn't have any medication for sleeping. I received no psychiatric treatment or even counseling, beyond what Jeff Redmond offered. I just quit meth cold turkey.

My medicine was church. I just spent a lot of time at church. I attended the Bayside's college group, The Shore on Thursdays, on Friday nights I would go to the Bayside group for recovering addicts called Celebrate Recovery. On Sundays I attended morning worship services and on Tuesday night I went with Mom to the Breaking Free Bible study. Church became a substitute for drugs. It was so new to me and I just trusted God because church seemed to be working. Being busy with church activities helped keep me distracted from meth. I felt a new kind of awakening within me. I wasn't sure what it all meant, but it felt good to trust something besides the deceptive drugs to get me through the day.

I had grown up without God. After our brief stint as church members in elementary school, I became a hard core atheist. I had spent the last 15 years truly believing that there was no God. I thought that when I died, I'd be put in a box, placed in the ground and that was it. I had no interest in God, and I thought anyone who believed in a God was crazy.

Now, I was beginning to see that maybe there really was a God and maybe he really did love me. It was such a new idea, and after relying on meth for so long, I was ready to trust something with more promise. I felt a soft tug toward God and I wasn't sure what it was, but I wanted to learn more about him. It was as if I was awakening from a deep sleep and opening my eyes to a whole new world.

CHAPTER 15

WAKING UP

I was getting better. After three weeks into being clean, I was showing signs of getting well. I was so excited when one morning, I was able to get out of bed, take a shower and not be so tired that I had to go back to bed.

I called Mom at work. "Mom!" I shouted into the phone, "This is so great! I took a shower and didn't climb back in bed. I put on my makeup and styled my hair. I'm not too tired! It feels amazing!" It was exhilarating! When I was on drugs I believed that it would never again be possible to get up in the morning without smoking meth. I needed that instant energy boost to function. I would get up, smoke some meth, take a shower, smoke a little more meth, dry my hair, smoke a little more meth and then style my hair only to smoke more meth. Each step of getting ready in the morning was interrupted with smoking meth. Now I could get up and get ready with no meth! It was a huge victory for me. For the first time in a long time I felt truly awake!

I began to look forward to all the different Bayside nights. I really started to enjoy the Tuesday night Bible study with Mom and her friends. Her boyfriend, Dillon gave me my own Bible and I started to really study it. If I had questions, I'd ask Mom. She was a relatively new Christian and often we would ask Dillon for answers. Dillon would pull out his glasses from a drawer in Mom's kitchen and sit down with me to help me understand. I'd read a bit more, and always had so many questions. Dillon was so patient, helping me to grasp the concepts of a loving God who really cared about me. I continued to attend The Shore on Thursday nights and Celebrate Recovery on Friday nights. Of course Mom and I also attended worship at Bayside on Sunday.

I kept studying my Bible and whenever I couldn't understand something, I'd ask a lot of questions.

"You have to read and reflect," Dillon told me. I didn't have a clue about most of what I'd read, but I was very curious and as I read, there was sort of an awakening happening within my spirit. I felt so broken. I knew that I needed something. I didn't know what I needed, but I knew I needed something.

As I continued to get well, I decided that I should start looking for a job. I liked earning my own money and being responsible for myself. I could even get myself ready in the morning without taking a break between steps! I felt myself getting stronger, but I knew I had a long way to go.

I was still very rocky in my recovery. Cognitively, I desperately wanted to remain clean, but the craving for meth was unbearable. I called my mom or Jeff Redmond from Bayside, four and five times a day, begging for support and afraid that I wouldn't be able to resist the pull of the drugs. Often I felt as if I would pull my hair out and that I was crawling inside my own skin.

During those first few weeks of being off drugs, believe it or not, I was still talking to Jackson. Despite the brutal treatment and threats to kill me, I had been talking with him on the phone, and telling him about my new life.

I also called Emilio. He was out of prison again and since I was so excited that I was clean from drugs, I wanted to share that good news with him. Emilio always wanted me to come to the Bay Area to visit him, but since I didn't have a car, and I knew Mom would never take me to see him, that wasn't possible.

Deep inside I knew that staying away from both Jackson and Emilio was the smart thing to do. They both had been major players in my drug use over the years. Being clean felt so good. I didn't want to risk my new found recovery. Yet, inexplicably, I found myself being pulled back toward them.

CHAPTER 16

AN INVITATION TO SOMETHING SPECIAL

At The Shore one Thursday night, I learned that there was a three day retreat coming up. The agenda sounded amazing and I was excited. I really wanted to attend. But then I learned that it cost $200 to participate. I didn't have $200. I didn't have $20! But all my friends at Bayside encouraged me to go.

That night, when I got home, I told Mom about the retreat. "It sounds awesome!" I told her. "John Harris will be speaking. It's up at Lake Tahoe, and you know how much I love it up there!" It felt good to feel enthusiastic about something again.

Mom asked me a few questions about the retreat, like who I'd drive up with and how long we'd be gone, and just some of the details, as she perused the retreat brochure. Then she surprised me when she said, "Erin, I think you should go. I'll pay for it."

The retreat rolled around and I was excited. On the day of departure, I was 40 days clean and a breath away from relapse most of those 40 days. I had physically purged the drugs from my body and the withdrawal symptoms had subsided some. But it had taken me every day of that 40 day period to regain my strength, just to be able to get up and shower in the morning and still have enough energy to go throughout the day and be back in bed by 9 p.m. It had been a painful process.

Even though I knew I was getting better, stronger and healthier, I was aware that I was still an addict, craving meth and tackling my addiction from moment to moment. I didn't know how I was going to get through three days of this retreat, with meth still pulling me away from my focus.

Bayside had planned for various car pools to meet at the church and depart at four different times throughout the day. I was scheduled to ride with some new friends and depart at 11 a.m. but when I arrived for that departure, the car I planned to ride in was full. I was so disappointed, but this guy driving another car said, "Hey, you can ride with me." I didn't know his name, but I accepted his offer and climbed in the backseat of his SUV. I looked around and there were three of us, me, him and another girl. I didn't know either of them.

They were both friendly enough and I relaxed in the back seat, prepared to enjoy a quiet drive through the foothills into the Sierra Mountains on California highway 50. The driver popped a CD in and said, "Let's listen to this CD."

I sat back, expecting music and was surprised that it was a lecture tape about evolution versus creation. All my life I had been a hard core atheist. "Oh great," I thought. "Evolution versus creation – this ought to be good. I'm an evolutionist!"

But I sat back and listened as we started up the steep climb into the Sierra as the speaker was talking logically and rationally about science in a way that I had never considered before. "This is crazy!" I thought, because, me, the evolutionist was agreeing with the speaker. The guy on the CD was making really good points, explaining how certain atoms are impossible to evolve and how traditional evolutionary science was wrong.

As I looked out the car window at the amazing views of the Sierra foothills, I was astounded. "Damn! This is crazy! This guy is actually making sense!" I thought over and over again. I was fascinated with this lecture and surprised when we drove up to our destination. We didn't even get to finish the CD. "I need a copy of that CD," I told the driver.

"All right I can do that for you." He answered.

We checked in and the leaders of the program were expecting me. I was struggling to remain clean and they knew that and were there to support me. Bayside had lots of rules for the trip which included no substances, including cigarettes. While I was off meth, I still smoked cigarettes and before I bought my ticket I had explained to Raelynn that I would have to be allowed to smoke cigarettes occasionally if I went on the retreat.

"Don't worry about it," Raelynn told me. "Do what you need. I'll be your accountability," she told me. Since I was very new to The Shore, Raelynn arranged for me to room with someone I was acquainted with named Corrina. The lodge was a two story hotel, but I discovered that I wasn't in one of those rooms. I was going to stay in the cabins instead. Raelynn took me outside and pointed up a steep, snow-covered hill where about a mile up there in the woods I would find my room.

So I started my ascent up the mountain, dragging my rolling suitcase through the snow, over the rocky trail in my high heel boots. It was February, in the Sierra Mountains at about 7,000 foot elevation and I was freezing by the time I arrived at the cabin. I tumbled in the door and tossed my things on an unclaimed bed. I looked around. I didn't know anyone in the room.

Friday was our first night and it was interesting. While most of the kids were all staying in a fine hotel, my roommates and I were in rustic cabins with little heat and cold showers. The hike up and down that hill was a challenge. I decided to make the best of it. Our first event was going to be held in the worship center at 7 p.m. But the last group of travelers hadn't arrived yet so they pushed the start time back to 8 p.m. to include everyone. I'd been visiting with the girl in the bed next to mine named Allyson and she and the other six girls and I just chilled in our room, waiting for the evening's events to begin.

At 8 p.m. we all hiked down the hill in the dark to find the worship room set up sort of like a mini version of Bayside's sanctuary. There was a stage in front of a big room, and I noticed that they'd even brought the colored spot lights that highlighted the band. The floor was carpeted and there were rows of chairs lined up, with an aisle in the middle. I saw a projector and a big screen up front and a table in the back loaded with refreshments, coffee, soft drinks and water. It was a very cozy worship room and I began to relax and feel at home.

Finally everyone arrived and we began our opening worship. The band began to play the music that I loved from The Shore, and all 100 college-age attendees began to worship God together. I loved this part of The Shore each Thursday night back at Bayside. But tonight, it was different, better and unreal. The music and the words to the songs seemed to wrap around me. I was already raising my hands during worship back at Bayside, but tonight I felt as if God was reaching back toward me. I can't totally describe it, but something was definitely unusual as we sang our familiar songs and listened to the music.

The worship was supposed to be an hour long service, but we were all so caught up in the holiness of the service that we continued to sing and praise God for about three and a half hours! At one point, one of the leaders told us to take off our shoes, because we were standing on holy ground. I looked around in wonder and thought, "What is going on here?"

Pastor Brian Orme gave a message during the service that was very spiritual and touched my heart. The music, the message, the scripture, the fellowship – all of it was different and I felt so blessed to be part of it.

I kept worshiping with the others, and inside I was marveling. "This is crazy stuff. Cool, but really weird." I trusted the leaders of the worship and I was totally going with whatever they said.

It was an emotionally moving and an extremely spiritual worship time. I had never experienced this kind of passionate worship before, but oh wow, I loved it. Everyone just stayed, singing, standing, some on their knees; a hundred kids, all focused on glorifying a God that I was just beginning to realize existed, let alone loved me. It was amazing. By the time we were dismissed, I was exhausted, but exhilarated. I felt my soul awaken and my heart open.

When we got back to the cabin I called Mom, "This is phenomenal!" I told her excitedly. "I've never experienced anything like this! It's the most amazing experience I've ever had."

Mom asked me a couple questions, but instead of answering her I just kept bubbling over with enthusiasm. "These people are great! They like me. They make me feel included, and the worship service tonight was awesome!"

When I settled into bed that night I reflected back on the night. It had been amazing and very different from anything I had expected or ever experienced before.

The next morning was Saturday and we all met for breakfast and then on to another session in the worship hall. Pastor John Harris was there and the first thing he did was begin to talk about the previous night.

"I've never experienced anything like that before," he told us. Then he asked people to stand up and tell what God had been doing in their lives. People started getting up left and right, walking to the microphone and telling their stories.

Something inside was saying to me, "Erin, go up there." And I kept answering back, "No way! You're tripping! I'm not going up there!"

But a nagging little voice inside kept saying, "Go up there."

Inside I answered that voice, "If you want me to go, you'll show me. I'm not going up there without a sign."

My roommate, Allyson, kept giving me the elbow. "You should go up there!" she encouraged me enthusiastically.

"You're crazy," I whispered to her. "I'm not telling 100 people I'm a drug addict! It's not happening!"

And then I stood up.

I sat down. I thought, "What the heck is going on? I'm not going."

My new friend, Richie was at the podium and he looked out and said, "You're going. You're next."

"Oh my god! I can't do this!" I told Allyson, as I got up to go toward the microphone.

When I got up to the podium, I saw Brian Orme in the back of the room listening to everybody. Pastor John Harris put his arm around me and handed the microphone. I still didn't know what I was going to say!

I looked at the microphone and gulped. "Hi, I'm Erin; I've only been going to The Shore for a couple weeks. I've been struggling with drug addiction and today I am 40 days sober."

Then I stopped when I realized I'd just told 100 people that I was a drug addict. What had I done?

But something strange happened. People started cheering for me. I could hardly believe it. These were "church people" and I expected them to judge me. Instead they started cheering and clapping for me!

"I don't really know God very well," I continued. "I feel like I'm not worthy of his love because of my past. But I'm grateful to be here and last night was amazing."

I handed the microphone back to the pastor and went back to my seat.

We adjourned to small groups of eight to 10 people with a leader. I didn't know what was going to happen now, since I'd just told the whole assembly that I was a drug addict.

There was a topic to discuss and everyone was still talking about their experience the night before in the worship service. When it got to my turn, I sort of repeated that I was interested in knowing God, but that I didn't feel worthy. It made me uneasy because I didn't know how to have a relationship with God.

The entire group was very supportive, and prayed with me. Then we ended that session and we had an afternoon of shopping and exploring South Tahoe. A few of the girls and I went into town, got coffee and were just having fun hanging out. We came back to the lodge for dinner and then to evening worship.

The band played again and we had a time of praise and worship. Then Brian Orme got up to speak. To my surprise he called me and another guy to come up to the front.

I was sitting in my seat, not anticipating anything like this. I looked around and everyone was nodding, encouraging me to go up there. I got up thinking, "Okay.... What's going on?"

When I got up there, Brian told me and the other guy, "I just want you to know everybody is worthy of God's love. He doesn't judge. Your past means nothing to him. Jesus is your savior and he died on the cross for your sins. You are forgiven."

I took a deep breath. That sounded really good to me. Then Brian asked, "Can I pray over you?"

I smiled with a trembling lower lip and nodded. The guy up there with me agreed as well. Brian put his right hand on my head and his left hand on the other guy's head. He invited some other people to come up and put their hands on me too. There were several people crowded around us, all trying to touch me.

And then Brian began to pray. I don't know what he said, but when he started praying, I just started bawling. Not quietly crying, not sobbing shyly; I began hysterically bawling.

As Brian prayed, I cried. I was so broken. I felt as if I were broken into a hundred thousand little pieces. Sort of like when you see windshield glass shattered along the road, and there are thousands of tiny pieces that can never be put back together again. That's how shattered my life was. I was crushed physically, emotionally, mentally and spiritually.

I could hear the music playing in the background as Brian prayed and I could feel the hands of the other believers. It was warm in the room and I remember that I was wearing jeans, a "wife beater" tank top and a Volcom sweatshirt. I could hear Brian's voice, but I couldn't understand the words. As Brian continued to pray, I began to sense the music beat within me and I felt as if the bass and drums of the band were pulsating inside me.

And then I experienced the most amazing phenomenon of my life. As Brian continued to pray, it started to feel like something was being pulled right out of me. I had the sensation that a vacuum was sucking something out of my body. The music continued to play but all I could hear was Brian's voice and the bass of the band. The percussion beats were pounding inside me and I began to tingle all over. Then, gloriously, it felt as if something was being pulled out of the top of my head, right where Brian's hand was.

Brian finished his prayer and asked the leadership team from The Shore to get in two lines. He invited all the worshipers to walk through the line. The members of the leadership team touched each one of us and prayed for us individually. I was awe-struck. I didn't know for sure what had happened, but I knew that I was spiritually awakened and I had been part of something amazing. I knew it came from God.

Brian and I talked a bit and I explained what I had felt. "Thank you for praying for me," I told him with tears in my eyes. The service ended and everyone chatted a bit, polishing off the last of the refreshments and then we began to break up and head back to our rooms for the night.

The girls in my room and I stayed up pretty late that night in the cabin, talking. The girls were so friendly and I was really enjoying their company. When we finally went to bed, and the lights went out, I looked up at the ceiling and sighed. I felt at peace. I didn't know what it was, but I knew that something was different. I'd found hope; I'd become a believer. I was wrapped in Christian principles and I knew I was a child of God.

CHAPTER 17

RECOGNIZING MY MIRACLE

Sunday morning of the retreat, I woke up and felt distinctly different. I felt like something had been lifted off my shoulders. Oddly, there was no desire to smoke meth.

For the past 40 days, I had awakened every morning scared. Each day had dawned with fear, facing another day of temptation to use meth. But this morning, I woke up hungry, feeling less pressure and looking forward to the day.

The girls and I all got up and went to breakfast. Everyone was chatting about the retreat and making plans to return home that day. I joined in the conversations and noticed that I was more relaxed than I'd been in a very long time. I knew that I felt different; I had no desire to smoke. Instead of being consumed with fear that today might be the day I would fall back into drug use, I experienced the freedom of looking forward to a day without even thinking of drugs.

After I got home, I continued to escape the craving for the deadly meth. I went from calling people for support several times a day to not calling anyone, because I had no desire for drugs at all. I wasn't even thinking about using drugs anymore! What was even more interesting was that the anxiety and nervousness of missing drugs was gone. I didn't twitch and I no longer felt as if there were bugs under my skin. All the physical traits of a drug addict in rehab were gone. I was fully awakened from the nightmare of the drug world.

I wish I could say that I realized with a bang that all these changes had happened miraculously at the retreat. My reality was that God was so new to me; it took a few days before I realized that this new absence of drug addiction was real. Most startling was when I realized that it was truly of God.

When Brian had prayed for me and I'd felt that sensation of something being pulled out of the top of my head, I knew that God had put his hand on me. It was so personal and such an intimate connection with a God that I had barely known, that I didn't claim it as a miracle immediately. I was a drug addict and I'd done terrible things in the quest for more drugs. How could the loving God everyone was telling me about, give me this kind of gift, when I barely new him?

I had a newfound desire to know God and I immersed myself in scripture, prayer and worship. Each day I'd wake up, almost expecting the old meth cravings to descend upon me, only to realize that I no longer had any drug cravings. At first I'd think, "Oh, maybe this is just a good day," as I began to get dressed without a struggle to reach for a meth pipe. I was relieved to discover that every day was becoming a "good day" and I began to hope that this was real.

Someone at Bayside approached me about telling my story with a video. They were planning to use five different personal stories for a "My Story" series on how Bayside church works in people's lives. The guy who talked with me told me there would be features on kids, marriage, me and something else. We sat down together and he told me that he wanted to make a video about my healing. I was willing to share my story if it would help and encourage others. He had me fill out a questionnaire and then he lined a professional video crew to produce a five minute first person story of my addiction and healing. It was supposed to be one of several stories shown for a Vision Desserts event, and I was surprised when at the service they just showed my story. I was more surprised by how everyone at church referred to what happened to me as a miracle. It was then that I started to think that my experience was indeed a miraculous healing from God.

The following week, they showed the video about my story to over 3000 people at worship services. And since then the video has been seen around the world. Today, people recognize me from that film. Randomly, people will come up to me in the grocery store, at work or at church, encouraged by seeing how God has worked in my life. It has given me new confidence that I really was chosen to receive a miracle of healing from drug addiction by God; and that I have a responsibility to use it for his glory. I know now that this truly was a miracle and I want to move forward in God's plan for me, and show people that it's possible to be healed from drug abuse.

I began to understand that God had his hand in what I have come to realize was a healing. With each day dawning with drug-free grace, it became clear that I had received the gift of a miracle from God.

I was humbled beyond belief as I recognized and honored God for his glory and grace. As weeks went by, I began to not even think about drugs or worry that I might be tempted to try drugs again. I continued to meet with Jeff Redmond, and to attend Celebrate Recovery services at Bayside, The Shore, Bible study and Bayside worship services regularly. I also joined a national 12 step program. As I regained my strength, my old personality began to emerge and I felt my ambitions return.

My one, sad and aching regret was the loss of my relationship with my younger sister Erica and my dad. I called my dad and tried to tell him about my recovery. I was so excited about being clean and not needing drugs anymore. I remember saying, "Dad, today I'm two whole months clean!"

My Dad had been through so much with me he wouldn't allow himself to believe in me again. "Call me when you're two years clean," he said and hung up the phone.

Erica had been equally hurt by my drug use and all the behaviors that went with it. We had been so close as children but once drugs took over my life, Erica became my best co-dependent. She would help me out, give me money or whatever I needed. But even Erica's love for me was pushed to the limit and she removed herself from my life. Now that I was clean and recovering, I called Erica over and over again, but she would never pick up her phone or call me back. I understood that she wouldn't want to talk to me when I was using drugs, but I couldn't understand why she didn't want to talk to me now that I was clean and ready to be her sister again.

Mom kept encouraging me. "Just pray about it," Mom said. "God will turn their hearts when the time is right."

"The time is now!" I cried. The tears poured down my face in frustration, hurt and humiliation and I knew that I was solely responsible for creating this discord.

I continued to call both of them regularly; leaving messages, trying to sound cheerful and always hoping that I would get a call back from Dad or even just a text message from Erica. It seemed hopeless after awhile, but I took Mom's advice and continued to pray about it, and to make regular attempts to show both my dad and Erica that I was healed. I was clean and I was definitely going to stay that way.

Then one night, I called Erica and left a message and a few minutes later, she called me back. I was so thrilled to hear from her and we began to mend our friendship. We talked for over an hour and it was exhilarating to laugh with my sister, almost like when we were children. I could tell Erica was skeptical, but she was talking to me and I promised God that I would not ever let her down again.

Eventually, even my dad's heart softened toward me, and we were able to regain a semblance of a father-daughter relationship. I knew that I had hurt my dad deeply and that he might not ever truly accept me back as the daughter he once loved, but I was determined to work on that relationship with prayer, living a clean lifestyle and staying in touch.

As I grew stronger, and healthier, I became restless just sitting at home. I decided that I wanted to go back to work. I appreciated all Mom had done to help me in recovery, but I was 22 years old and I needed to be independent and on my own. I polished up my resume' and began to interview for a new job. God was becoming my friend and I began to trust him to open doors for me. I kept thinking of that Bible verse from the twenty-ninth chapter of Jeremiah that Jeff Redmond had told me the very first day I went to Bayside, "For I know the plans I have for you," declares the Lord, "plans to prosper you and not to harm you, plans to give you hope and a future."

It excited me to think that God really had plans for me. I had goals again. I wanted to get back into a good job and I was hopeful that I could meet a wonderful man to share my life and my new found faith. I started to talk to God about it, "God, if you have plans for me, you'll arrange it. I'm ready."

One night after a meeting at The Shore, I wasn't feeling well and I left early. Outside in the courtyard, I met Brady, a really good looking guy who had just moved to our area from Los Angeles. We chatted a bit and he told me that he was a member of an alcoholic support group. I laughed, "Oh, me too!" He grinned and said, "Hey, we should go to a meeting together sometime."

We exchanged numbers and the next week he took me to a meeting. Soon we began dating and it was so sweet to have a relationship with someone who wasn't on some kind of substance all the time. I started to think that Brady just might be my Mr. Right. The first six months of our relationship were amazing.

However, to my dismay, Brady relapsed and got back into drugs. I was angry, hurt and trying to hard to help him. Watching Brady's mother cry over his lies and mood swings broke my heart. It was a shock for me to now be on the flip side of drug addiction – I began to understand what I'd put my parents and sister through.

I was in love with a guy on drugs and I kept asking the same questions of him that my parents had asked of me. "Why can't you get clean? Why are you lying? Why are you so angry all the time?" Brady developed a big attitude and an arrogance I hadn't seen before. He stopped going to church because he was mad at God. The more I struggled with Brady's addiction, the more I realized how devastating it was for my parents to deal with me all those years. As much as I loved him, I held my ground.

I stayed clean throughout Brady's relapses and tried to help him and his family. Brady would get off drugs for a couple months, but then lapse back into the old patterns. He'd get clean and then go back on drugs. As Brady struggled, I found myself getting stronger and stronger, more resolved to never return to that life style.

Brady's addiction was an eye-opener for me because Brady would lie to me about using, and I could tell instantly that he was using and lying. Now I could see that I couldn't hide drug use from those who loved me. Brady thought he was hiding it from me so well, but I knew that when he was nodding off on the couch that he was high, not just tired. I knew that he was using when he was loud, mean or angry. Being the recipient of his lies, possessiveness, unwarranted anger and paranoia, made me realize what I'd put my family through all those years. I was truly humbled by the fact that my mom had hung in there with me through recovery.

It took me a year to finally pull away from Brady. By that time he'd gotten clean again and stayed clean for about a month, but so much damage had been done in our relationship that it wasn't the same. I knew that Brady couldn't possibly be the man God had planned for me to spend my life with or to be the father of my children.

After 18 months, with 12 of them being the victim of Brady's addiction, I'd had enough of being in love with a drug addict. I really thought God had put Brady in my life to be my soul mate. Instead, I was beginning to think that God had put Brady in my life to show me the opposite end of drug addiction – how it hurts those who love you even more than it hurts you. Despite Brady's promises, I stopped being his co-dependent and ended the relationship. As an addict, I should have recognized all the signs and symptoms, but God let me go through this process on my own. It was painful, but I'm grateful to have left that relationship with valuable lessons and confirmation that I never want to be associated with an addictive lifestyle again. It's not part of God's plan for me.

CHAPTER 18

THE FUTURE IS MINE TO CLAIM

As I grew better acquainted with God, I began to realize that my miracle of healing from drug addiction was uncommon. Professionals in drug treatment commented that my experience was extremely unusual and truly miraculous. I came to realize that God had chosen me to receive a divine healing. Sometimes I wondered why. Why did God choose me for such an amazing physical and spiritual experience? Why did he put me among the exact people that I needed to reach for him? Why did he love me so much that he redeemed me from all that I'd lost? I didn't have answers, but as I came to understand all that God had done for me, I felt a responsibility to use these gifts from God.

I began to focus on all that was good in my life. My gentle awakening had grown to a fully active, alert relationship with the God who had created me. I was healthy again, regaining my spunk and getting stronger physically, mentally and emotionally. I was working as a server at a restaurant, making great money, and enjoying my new sober friends. I had no desire to see any of my old friends from my drug life. I was learning a lot about God, studying the Bible and learning to live substance free. It was invigorating and I thanked God with every breath.

One night I got home from work and looked at my life. I liked what I saw. I liked the clear blue eyes that stared back at me in the mirror, the long glossy locks of hair that fell into soft curls around my face. I liked the glow of my skin and the relaxed countenance that surrounded me. But it just wasn't enough. I was a goal setter, a long-range planner and I wanted a career. Mom was working late in her home office, and I stopped by the door.

"Mom, I need to talk."

Mom turned from her computer and smiled. It was good to see her smile when I started a serious conversation. After all the times I'd been in trouble or needed money or help from drug consequences, it warmed my heart to see her smiling at me not knowing what I might want. "What's up?" she asked warmly.

"I don't know what to do with my life," I told her. "I've messed up so many times. I don't know how to plan."

Mom kept smiling, and replied, "Let's put that behind us, Erin. You've received this gift from God, and you are doing so well. Let's just focus on what he has planned for you."

I gulped. "That's just it. I don't know what to do with my life," I told her.

She stayed positive, "Well, what do you love?" Mom asked.

"Well, I have a passion for fashion and I'm kind of interested in forensics," I told her.

"That's an interesting combination," Mom laughed.

"I know, but I want to *do* something with my life," I told her. "I'm afraid that if I don't do something now, I'm just going to work at the restaurant and come home to watch television for the rest of my life."

"Well, what do you want to do?" Mom asked me. She didn't skip a beat. She didn't give me any warnings or caution me about taking on too much too soon. She just put it out there for me to describe.

"I want to go to school." I said timidly. "But I'm afraid."

"Afraid of what?" Mom asked.

"I'm afraid to fail," I admitted. "I've failed so many times, at so many things, I'm afraid that if I start school, I'll fail."

Mom reached out and grabbed my hand. "You're not going to fail if you have a plan."

"Do you really think I can do it?" I asked. Her encouragement meant so much to me. My mom knew better than anyone how badly I had messed up my life. She knew how hard it had been to get to this new stage of my life. "I don't want to just spend the rest of my life working at a restaurant, settling for less than I can really do."

"Okay, then let's find a school," Mom told me and turned around to her computer and we started searching on the internet for forensic programs and fashion schools.

For the next few days I spent every opportunity I had, looking for a place to help me reach a career goal. I was still fearful of taking on too much, too soon. I hadn't ever really been a good student and I knew going back to school would be hard. It was unknown and I had done nothing but fail for the last two years, and I didn't want to fail again.

I discovered a fashion school in Sacramento, and made an appointment with an admissions counselor. I drove out to the International Academy of Design and Technology and discovered a fashion design and marketing major. This was exactly the training I needed to become a buyer.

I left the session, and called my mom from the parking lot.

"Mom!" I shouted into the phone. "You have to come to this school, right now!"

Mom was laughing on the other end of the line. "Where are you? What do you want to study?" she asked joyfully.

"I want to go to fashion school," I said boldly. "I was good at retail at Luxx. I loved it. I want to become a professional in the fashion industry! I want to be a buyer for Nordstrom."

A week later I started at IADT. I was ready to study for a career as a fashion design and marketing major in January of 2009, just two years past my miracle healing. Just 18 months later, I achieved an Associates Degree and began an exciting internship in fashion marketing. It felt so good to be taking my gifts from God and working toward something that I knew pleased him. My career goal was to become a corporate buyer for a store like Nordstrom.

CHAPTER 19

DISCOVERING WHO I AM

*W*hen I went to The Shore retreat where I experienced my
healing from drug addiction, I wasn't a fully committed
Christian. I was more in a "curious mode" at that stage of my faith. I had
been introduced to Jesus that first morning I met with Jeff Redmond at
Bayside and I knew God was working in my life. But it was all so new,
and combined with the withdrawal symptoms of meth addiction, I had a
lot of sensations that I couldn't always associate with God. I think I was
experiencing a tender awakening of my spirit.

After my experience at the retreat, I became much more convinced
that God was acting in my life. As a result, I became much more involved
with God. I knew things were changing in my life because I was going to
church and forming a relationship with God. I could easily see that my life
was improving because of God and I had no problem giving him the credit
for all the good things that were happening to me since I'd met him. I was
still going to the Bible study by Beth Moore, called "Breaking Free," where
I learned who God is and what he wanted for me. Each week I read all the
scriptures that were required and which sparked a lot of questions for me
at Bible study.

I believed that God loved me, but I still had all those non-believer questions like, "Why do bad things happen to good people?" or "Why do children suffer or get sick?" or "Why do innocent people get beaten or robbed?" I still had questions, but I was open to learning and understanding from the perspective of a believer. I wasn't a full-force Christian yet, but I was definitely exploring it and my soul was roused and curious.

Each week, when I'd go to The Shore, the pastors quoted scriptures and then spoke on them. I started going home and reading the whole chapter in the Bible where I found that scripture. It wasn't always easy to understand with all the symbolism, and the unfamiliar history, but I dug deep in my Bible. I asked a lot of questions and people were always so kind and patient with me as I began to understand the basic tenets of being a child of God.

As I continued to study and learn more about God, I encountered more people who would ask how my recovery was going. So many people at church had been praying for me, that it was common for people to just ask, "How are you? How's your recovery going?"

When people found out that I wasn't in a treatment facility, that I hadn't suffered any of the long-term health effects or addictive ticks of a meth user, the prevailing comment was always, "Oh! Praise God! That's a miracle." Even professionals at a local teen drug treatment center commented that my experience was indeed unusual and miraculous. When health care professionals, steeped in science, began to call my healing divinely ordained, it gave me something new to think about.

I honestly don't know if I ever would have thought of my experience as a miracle on my own. I knew that what happened at the retreat hadn't been a normal experience, but until I had so many people talk about it being a miracle, I just thought of the experience as if it were unusual.

I was grateful for the gift of healing and willing to help and encourage others. I became a sponsor in an addiction support group and I felt chosen to help other girls from my experience. But I didn't really feel called to become a drug rehab counselor or to spend my life helping others with addiction. I felt God calling me away from drugs and to be the person I was meant to be. I want to help people in other ways. I know that God can comfort, heal and repair lives on many levels.

But I do feel called to dedicate my life to serving God. I feel very humble by my experience and I want to walk with the Lord all my days. What I don't want to do is center my life around addiction. For me, drug addiction was something that happened and now it's all changed. I feel that if I went into counseling, I'd stay sick to a degree.

What I really want is to be the person God created me to be.

After having been awakened by God, I am confident that he wants me to be that loud, outgoing, goofy, sometimes crazy girl who waves her arms when she talks and laughs out loud at the silliest things. I want to take this gift of healing and use all the other gifts God has given me to be a totally new person.

I learned a lot from two nationally recognized 12 step programs. They were very therapeutic and helpful toward repairing a lot of relationships in my life. After I realized that I'd been healed, I elected to leave both groups because I found so many of the people were just angry. Some of them were so mad at the world and a support group was just a substitute for the alcohol or drugs. I don't want my identity to be wrapped up in anger or depression. That's not me.

The real me is strong, creative, responsible, and a total capitalist. I am a money-motivated person. I want to have a career and make money, have nice things, and move forward. I don't want to be "Erin, the former drug addict." I just want to be "Erin." I'm open to sharing the wonderful miracle of how I was reborn and given a second chance on life, with anyone who will listen.

The girlfriends I have now are a mix of girls from church and girls from work. We hang out often and they are all very respectful of my story. Sometimes we go out to have fun and dance the night away. Once in awhile they'll drink, but I never touch a drop of alcohol and they know they can count on me to be the designated driver.

CHAPTER 20

ME AND MY DAD

*I*ve always known that my father loved me. But for most of my pre-teen, teen and adult years, Dad and I didn't see eye to eye on anything. I was an out-of-control child in high school, and despite my parents' attempt at discipline, I challenged every rule and every consequence Dad put before me. No matter what tactics my dad tried, no matter how uncomfortable he made my choices, no matter what he took away, I continued to challenge him.

So looking back, I think it's understandable that things were never great between Dad and me for most of my life. Once I was healed from drug addiction and began living clean, Dad and I developed a better relationship.

When I was a child, I didn't know that Dad was an alcoholic, but it was clear that he drank every day. As I got older, I figured out that he was drinking to excess and I noticed the behavior changes in Dad as soon as he was under the influence of his favorite liquor. However, I didn't think it was a problem. My parents were both employed and financially successful. My sister and I were busy, doing our own things, and I didn't think alcoholism was an illness, but simply that sometimes being with Dad was good, and sometimes not so good. I knew that the major reason Dad and I didn't get along was just because I questioned everything he said to me. I thought our conflicts were mainly because of my strong personality and my smart mouth.

Living clean and sober made me keenly aware how precious life is. It gave me a renewed sense of family and a yearning for strong relationships. After I became clean, my whole outlook on life changed. I began to appreciate life so much more than I ever did before. Today, when I wake up - I'm happy, and I'm loud, and I'm goofy. I celebrate my life every day, with fun, enthusiasm and energy. My friends' comments are often, "You're so crazy," or "What's wrong with you? Why are you so happy?" but that's just how I feel – filled with joy and it's bursting out of me. And I cherish every day that I have.

I also now treasure the relationships in my life, especially those within my family. And that's odd, because as a teenager, I didn't value my family much at all. I just wanted to get away from them. I moved out on my own at 18 and spent the next five years running from the ones who loved me most. Now I care deeply about family.

My father was the last person to believe that I really was off drugs for good. He had moved to Oregon after the divorce from my mom, but he had distanced himself from me more than just geographically. He was also emotionally distant. His doubt about my ability to stay clean hurt me, but I kept calling him every day, reminding him that I loved him and that I was living clean. But sadly, Dad was not interested in me or my new strength and commitment to living drug free. It killed me that Dad wasn't interested in my life, but I knew that it was understandable since I had failed so many times. Dad thought this was another empty promise; another pledge I couldn't or wouldn't keep - like I had made to him so many times before.

I continued to call Dad every day, reminding him that I loved him and doing my best to describe my life without drugs. Mom kept telling me to be patient, that Dad would come around, but it hurt me deeply that I wasn't able to share all the new exciting things in my life with him.

And then, one day, finally, Dad called me back. We chatted for a bit, and that was the beginning of a rebuilding of our relationship. He decided to return to California to be near my sister Erica and me. That's when our relationship took off. We began to spend time together, and we met for lunch at least once a week.

Dad knew that part of my recovery included a national anonymous support group and attending church. I was hopeful that Dad would get help with his drinking through an alcohol counseling program. I felt confident that I could provide an avenue for Dad to find information for himself with my resources. Dad would question things I was doing all the time and he was interested in the 12 step program I had been involved with. He asked me lots of questions and he even met with a sponsor from a national alcohol support program.

I was thrilled. I thought that Dad was finally going to get help for his drinking. I had given him a book from my 12 step program and I would often find it open on his coffee table, so I knew he was reading it. I was super excited because I knew that Dad would be so much happier if he wasn't drinking all the time.

I loved this new relationship with my father. I had never been so close to Dad. We were sharing information and I was asking for his advice. Dad was talking to me about things we'd never talked about before. I talked with him about the guys I dated, and after awhile, Dad even talked with me about going into an alcohol rehab program. He told me that if I could find a good rehab center, he would go.

I was extremely happy to hear this and I began to pursue finding Dad a facility to get well. I was excited when I found a great place for him to go for treatment, but devastated when he backed out.

Dad knew that I was heavily involved in church. He wasn't interested in religion, but he respected the fact that it was through something at church that I was able to kick the drugs and get clean. Even though Dad wanted no part of religion, he attended a service at my church when they featured my story. He was impressed with the contemporary worship style of Bayside Church. He liked the upbeat music and the fact that the pastors made jokes and didn't wear clergy robes. But Dad would never take that first step toward the Celebrate Recovery Program at Bayside or any alcohol recovery support group.

For awhile things were good with Dad. He was looking for work, upbeat and positive and always excited to see me. But Alcoholism is a disease that progresses and wears on the body in many ways. Dad began to suffer pains in his legs and was unable to look for work. He became despondent and seriously depressed. I could see my dad spiraling into darkness and I was unable to stop it.

As life went on, Dad's drinking increased until about all he did was sit in his apartment, drink and smoke cigarettes. He became unpredictable, more deeply depressed and withdrawn. When my sister Erica wanted to get married, her fiancé went to talk to Dad to receive his blessing and permission. Dad gave them his blessing and promised to walk Erica down the isle.

Dad continued to withdraw as his disease progressed. It was the end of a semester and I was so busy with finals, projects and working that I hadn't been able to get over to see him on the same schedule as before. I was alarmed, when one day Dad sent me a text message. "Call me tomorrow. We have to talk."

I knew that Dad's funds were running low. He wasn't working and he wasn't on any kind of medical disability plan. I had an idea of how much money he might have left from the sale of his boat and house, and I was pretty sure that Dad's money was running out.

As near as I could tell, I thought that Dad had just about enough money left to make it through the end of June. Erica and I were on edge, concerned about Dad's depression, alcoholism and whatever the pain and numbness was that he was experiencing in both of his legs and feet. It was clear that Dad was extremely depressed and not doing well. I tried to talk to him about it, but Dad would just insist that he was fine.

My mom talked with Dad, explaining that Erica and I thought that Dad might end his own life. Erica and I went together to see him and said, "Dad, just tell us what you need. We'll help you." Each time our efforts were rebuffed. We had all sorts of conversations with Dad, trying to lead him to recovery. We talked with prevention specialists who told us that we were doing all the right things, but that we couldn't force Dad to do anything.

"Dad," I pleaded. "I know you're in a bad place. I know you don't know what to do with your life. I know you're having struggles. How can we change your situation?" I was willing to do anything for him.

Dad remained very closed. "I'm fine," he told me. "Don't worry about me.

I'm just fine." I had been so busy with the end of school semester craziness that Dad and I hadn't gone to lunch on the regular schedule. I was enrolled in 20 units, preparing for finals and completing some major projects, plus working and helping to plan Erica's wedding. I was swamped with very little time to do much else. When I did find time to meet with Dad, he didn't talk much, just said that he wasn't feeling well and that his feet hurt.

Final plans for Erica's wedding arrived amid my finals and major projects. Erica really hoped that Dad would walk her down the aisle, the way we had always played when we were little girls. But with both of us so busy, Dad was feeling left out. He and Erica had a phone argument that resulted with Erica feeling equally neglected and that manifested into my dad deciding not to attend the wedding. Three weeks before Erica's wedding sent Erica a text message that said, "We're done. Have a nice life."

It broke Erica's heart to have Dad miss her wedding. As I tried to console my sister, I continued to be concerned that about Dad's physical and emotional well being.

Four days after Erica's wedding, I got up like a regular day, went to the gym, and came home to get ready for school. I was just out of the shower, drying my hair, when I received a text message from Dad.

"What's your schedule today?" it said.

I thought, "Cool. Maybe he wants to go to lunch and talk." I sent a text back, "Through with school at 2:30 p.m."

"I'll be in tuf," the text came back. Dad often made spelling mistakes when he sent text messages because he would hit the wrong letters. I thought he meant in "town."

I sent a text right back, "Okay, do you mean you'll be in town? Do you want to do lunch?"

He sent a reply. "Sorry I'll text you in a few."

It was about 11:30 a.m. and I was in class when I received the next message from Dad. It scared me. "My life is all screwed up. I need you to pick up Sid before it gets crazy. I love you."

Sid was Dad's little dog and his constant companion. This message shot off an alarm. I tried to call Dad back, but he didn't pick up the phone. I called Erica and told her about the message and she was equally concerned.

I sent many messages to Dad, "Please pick up the phone." "I love you."

"What can I do to help?" These were all messages that I sent, hoping to get Dad's attention. Dad didn't pick up the phone or send a reply text.

Then suddenly, I received a text message from Dad, "I expect you to look after Sid. It's the least that you can do."

I knew what Dad was going to do, and I was helpless to do anything to stop it. I called and called Dad, but he didn't answer. Then I called for help - Mom promised to meet me at Dad's apartment and Erica started on her way from college, about six hours away. I hopped in my car to race toward Dad's apartment. I kept calling and calling Dad, with no answer.

"Please Dad," I cried through my fear, "Just answer your phone!"

Then suddenly I received a reply from Dad, "Please get Sid."

I kept driving; terrified that something was very wrong. I pulled into the apartment parking lot, and stopped in front of Dad's unit. I didn't want to go in by myself. I was afraid of what I might find.

I called the police. "I need an escort into my dad's apartment," I told the dispatcher. "I think he's going to kill himself."

I knew that Erica and Mom were both on their way to meet me here, and that the police would arrive soon, so I stood outside the gate of the apartment complex all by myself, watching for someone to come to help me.

I expected one police vehicle. What I saw was seven or eight squad cars swoop through the parking lot, lights flashing and sirens blaring.

"Which apartment is his?" the cop said as he jumped out of his car. I couldn't figure out what was going on. I pointed to Dad's apartment door. It was right by the gate.

"Are you Erin Kalte?" another officer asked me. I nodded. "I need to speak with you."

I started to take Dad's apartment key off of my key ring, and walk toward Dad's door. I expected a police officer to walk with me into Dad's apartment.

Instead the officer said to me, "Your dad is being rushed to UC Davis Medical Center."

I gasped and then I broke down in tears. I sat down on the curb. Neither Mom nor Erica were there, and I felt so alone and terrified sitting on the edge of the sidewalk. I curled into a ball and sobbed.

The officer continued, "Your father is suffering from a gunshot wound to the head."

Despite my shock and sadness, I started to wonder how the police officer knew this. "How do you know it's my dad?" I asked.

"We had a report of a man lying in the grass near Arco Arena. His identification matches your father's." was the reply.

"But how do you know this?" I asked trying not to believe what was happening. "How do you have all these details?"

Stunned, I sat on the on the curb, crying and crying. My emotions were wrapped into a wild ball of fury, sadness and disbelief. How could this happen?

The police went into Dad's apartment with a crime scene investigation team backing them up. Since the gun that was found at the scene of Dad's shooting only had two bullets in it, the police were concerned that there might be other victims in Dad's apartment.

"Do you know Dad's condition?" I asked the police officer.

"When ambulance reached him, he had a pulse and he was still breathing," was the reply.

That spurred me into action. "I need to go to the hospital." I stood up, reaching in my bag for my keys. "I need to go now!"

The police had more questions for me and I was stunned as a Crime Scene Investigating team began to go through Dad's apartment.

"Were you talking to your dad before it happened?" the officer asked me.

I pulled my phone out of my pocket and showed him the text messages. The police officer was reviewing the messages when one of the CSI members brought Sid out of the apartment. The little black Miniature Pincher was trembling and so frightened by all the confusion.

Mom arrived and tried to comfort me, but I was so angry and horrified that I rejected anything anyone had to share with me. "I need to go to UC Davis Med Center," I insisted. "I need to go now!"

But the police officer detained me, insisting that they needed more information from me. Finally, the police wrote the case number down, and allowed me to get into my car. The police and my mother both tried to stop me from driving in my emotional condition and offered to drive me to the hospital. Things were so out of control and all I wanted to do was handle the things I could control.

In my panicked state I screamed, "Don't comfort me! Don't talk to me! Don't touch me!" I got into my car and raced away. I drove the 10 miles to the hospital in minutes. Mom was in her car, right behind me.

I don't know what I was expecting when I got to the hospital. I knew that Dad had shot himself. I didn't know if he would survive but I thought that I would be able to see him if he was alive. I wanted to hold his hand, stroke his cheek and tell him I loved him. Most of all, I didn't want him to die alone.

I was like a wild woman at the hospital. I couldn't get anyone to listen to me about seeing Dad. After some shuffling of information, Mom and I were able to talk to the physician who took care of Dad when he arrived at the emergency room. A very young doctor came in to a small room and calmly stated, "I'm sorry to tell you, but your father shot himself in the head with nine millimeter gun. We lost him in the ambulance." I gasped and started to cry again. "We tried to resuscitate him here in the ER to get a heart beat. We gave him medication, but there was too much damage."

"I want to see him." I said firmly.

"No," Mom said.

I started screaming at Mom. "Don't tell me whether I can see my father!" I shouted. "I'll see my dad if I want to."

Mom tried to comfort me, "Erin, I know you are an adult. You make your own decisions. But think about this. Is that the last vision you want of your father?"

"Yes! It is." I was so angry, not at my mom, but at the whole situation. How could Dad do this to us? My rage was roaring in my head and I felt powerless to stop it.

I went outside the ER while the hospital arranged approval for me to see my dad's body. I called Erica who was still on the road and instructed her pull over so I could tell her what had happened. In the back of my mind I kept asking, "Why is this happening?" and "How is this real?"

I gave Erica the details as I knew them and told her that I was going in to see Dad one last time. Erica was crying with me over the phone. I told her

I would see her later, hung up the phone and went back into the emergency room waiting area.

A nurse led me to a closed door down a long hall. I entered a small room to find Dad's body, swollen and pale. There was a breathing tube still down his throat and his head was wrapped in bandages. I couldn't see the gun shot wound, just his face. A wave of grief wrapped in sadness, loss and wasted potential swept over me. I began to cry and sort of crumbled to the floor. I grabbed the bed post for support and as I looked up I could see Dad's clothing under the bed. His shoes were there, covered in blood.

I pulled myself up, collected my courage and touched Dad's cold, lifeless hand. Then I kissed my Dad's cheek. "I love you, Dad," I said. Then quietly, I said, "Goodbye." I walked out the door to find my mother waiting for me, and I fell into her arms and cried for about five minutes.

That night, Erica arrived back in Sacramento and she decided that she wanted to see Dad's body before cremation. I assumed my big sister role and accompanied Erica to a cold, sterile room. Erica and I tearfully said goodbye to Dad, with Mom in the wings. It was just as hard for me as the first time, but I could not let my little sister do this alone. After leaning on her for so many years, it comforted me to be a rock for my little sister once again.

The entire tragedy was so unreal. I thought being concerned about Dad's mental stability had been challenging, but it was nothing compared to dealing with his suicide. As his next of kin, I had to talk to the coroner and visit the crematorium. It was my job to go through Dad's personal effects, and execute his will and estate. Through most of it, I would find my mind wandering to wonder if it was reality or a nightmare that I could wake from.

I don't know where God was in all of this. I was so angry and terrified that I didn't think to pray as it was all crashing down around me. But I know that others were praying for me, petitioning God to get me through the deepest pain and horror I have ever experienced. I know that it was God who sustained me. For even in the face of my father's suicide, I stayed focused on life and I stayed clean. I completed my semester at college and kept my job. I have renewed confidence in my life plan and I am more convicted than ever that drugs have no place in my life. God remains my Lord.

As I reflect back on my father's illness, addiction and suicide, I recognize some parallels between us. Both my dad and I suffered from addiction and related illnesses. Both of us distanced ourselves from the very people who loved us most. Both of us denied that we had a problem, and both of us refused treatment. Both of us attempted to end our lives.

But that's where the parallels stop. When my suicide attempt failed, I found God, and God lead me through a miraculous journey that included healing, deliverance and peace. God moved me toward the help I needed. God is the focus of my life now, the giver of all things and the rock where I anchor my life.

Now instead of wanting to end my life, I wake up each day embracing the day and looking forward to the challenges that lie ahead. I am divinely inspired to carry out God's will in my life.

At the time of this writing, I continue to grieve for the loss of my father. I find myself reaching for the phone to call my dad for advice or for help in a minor crisis, like when the battery died in my car. I experience bursts of incredible sadness and other flashes of anger. The hurt in my heart lingers and sometimes I just want to be alone. Some moments are harder than others, but I talk to God about it, and he comforts me.

Through the tragedy of losing Dad, I have confirmation that my addition is healed. My ability to stay clean isn't just through the good times, but through the worst times as well. My miracle is real and I am a strong, divinely sustained, stable woman of God.

CHAPTER 21

ME AND GOD

*M*y walk with God is solid today. He's my best friend. Sometimes I find myself testing him. Not to see if he's real, but to see if I'm on the right track. It feels good to be at a point in our relationship that I can ask him, "So what's going on with this situation? What do you want me to do it fix it? Give me some direction."

Often I feel God smiling on me, as if to say, "Erin, I want you to have fun."

I have learned to relax in the presence of God. I'm secure in the fact that God and I have a special relationship. I take comfort in knowing that He loves me even if I slip and say a cuss word. That's just me. Today I try to include God in everything and I think he likes to laugh at me.

I definitely look to God as an authority, but also as a comfortable companion. He has all power, but I talk to him like he's my best friend asking things like, "Give me strength," or "Guide me through this." I can feel his presence whenever I talk to him.

My communication with God is two fold. I talk and he listens, but I've also learned to listen to him. God answers me often through my conscience. It's that "gut feeling" I get when I know something just doesn't feel right.

Often I ask him about something and later that day, I'll hear something or someone say something addressing the very thing I was looking to God for answers.

At one point after my healing, I was trying to decide if I should move out of my mom's house. I was well past the age when girls live with their parents. But I was still in school and there were good reasons to stay. I had been struggling with the decision if I should move out. My mom's advice was, "Let's pray about it and see where God directs us."

I had planned to move into a house with three girls. One of the three was the most dependable and the one who had been house hunting with me, and helping plan the finances. As I kept asking God to give me direction on this decision, this friend unexpectedly took a job in another city 100 miles away. I felt that God made it very clear that the time wasn't right for me to make a move just yet.

I also look for what Mom and I call "God Moments" all the time. Those are the times in our lives when things happen that others might call coincidence but we know that it's God showering us with gifts of wisdom, grace, love or whatever we need. I find "God Moments" all the time now, from simple things like finding my keys, to locating a school near my home to fulfill my career goal. I think of how God answered my prayer with Erica returning my call that first time, and I know that was a "God Moment" too. I always try to thank him for being present in those moments and I wrap myself in the comfort of his love each time.

Professionally I will practice a high standard of ethics. I was raised with high morals and when I was on drugs I left them all behind. But I've regained what I learned from Mom and Dad and now I practice values of personal integrity at all costs. Even little things can't be neglected. Recently I was putting all my purchases from Target into my car when I discovered that a can of hairspray wasn't in a bag, it was just wedged in the corner of the cart. I checked the sales slip, and sure enough, the clerk hadn't rung up the hairspray. I took hairspray back inside the store and the customer service rep was surprised when I asked her to ring it up. I couldn't just keep it – because God would know, and I don't want to do things that will disappoint him.

I also want to advance in the fashion industry. I want to be respected as a professional and to use my creativity, knowledge and hard work to carve out my niche in the fashion world. I like to take on the lead on projects, and I love leadership roles. I like to be in charge.

I plan a career as a motivational speaker. I have personal insight into so many confusing issues in the American culture and I want to use that to help others. Whether it's dealing with out of control teenagers, the losses associated with addiction, the death of a parent, suicide or just trying to fit in, I am open to sharing my point of view.

Eventually I want to marry and have a family, but Mr. Right, will have to understand that I'm very career motivated. I don't want to have kids before I'm 30. God has taught me a lot about men and what a man should be to a woman. I've learned that a secure man won't be threatened if I have a social life. My standards have skyrocketed since I left the drug world and I know that in the plan God has for me, he wants me to be with somebody who loves me for me, understands what I've been through and cherishes me. I believe that God chose me and allowed me to suffer through my addiction because he knew that I could handle it.

There's an old expression, "Whatever doesn't kill you, makes you stronger." For me, that statement is true. I've lived it. I have lived in the deepest, darkest pits of despair. In my short life, I've experienced losing everything I held dear. I've suffered the ravages of drug addiction and the withdrawal pain and gut wrenching cravings of being clean. I've known the desperation of attempting suicide and I've endured the agony of a parent's suicide. But with God's grace I have triumphed.

As a former meth addict, who tried to kill herself with methamphetamine overdose, I'm willing to use my past as something to help others; but I will not allow my former meth addiction to define me. God knew that I needed total healing. He allowed me to be so desperate that I tried to end my life. If I hadn't been as low as I was, I would never have come to him. So, if that's what it took for me to find God, then I think all that pain, suffering, humiliation and despair was worth it. I am honored to know my God, and to have been awakened to fulfill his plan for me.

As I reflect on the events I've outlined in this book, I am in awe of the many, many ways God protected me through my dark walk in the substance abuse world. As a drug addict, I assumed an incredibly risky lifestyle within a criminal culture. Yet I came out of that world relatively unscathed. Despite all of the crimes I committed, I have no criminal record. Throughout my addiction, unlike most female drug addicts, I never exchanged sex for drugs. Unlike most meth addicts, I have no physical scars, I didn't lose any teeth, and my hair and skin regained their healthy glow. I do not experience tics or nervous behaviors and I do not crave drugs.

I believe all of these blessings are part of that promise Jeff Redmond introduced me to at the lowest point of my addiction – that God has a plan for me. God sustained and protected me through that scary, dark behavior because he wanted me to fulfill his plan.

Today when I read Jeremiah 29:11, it means exactly the same as it did the first time I heard it. But now it's more than a promise, it's a fact. God does have a plan for me; I'm living proof. In the beginning of my healing, I was seeking God; now I've found Him. He is real and I will honor him with my life.

I believe that we are a culmination of our life experiences. I can either help people or hurt people with those experiences. If I choose to learn the lessons in those experiences, I can profit from them in all my relationships.

I know that being delivered from meth addiction was an unusual event and very special. But I am not the only person on earth who God has a plan for or who can receive a divine miracle. God loves everyone and he is ready to be Lord of all; you just have to ask him.

"For I know the plans I have for you," declares the Lord, *"plans to prosper you and not to harm you, plans to give you hope and a future."* Jeremiah 29:11

CELEBRATE RECOVERY

Celebrate Recovery is a nationally recognized Christian rehabilitation program that originated at Saddleback Church in Southern California. Programs are now offered around the world.

In 1996, Saddleback Church launched Celebrate Recovery with 43 people. It was designed as a program to help those struggling with hurts, habits and hang-ups by showing them the loving power of Jesus Christ through a recovery process. Celebrate Recovery has helped more than 7,500 people at Saddleback, attracting over 70% of its members from outside the church. Eighty-five percent of the people who go through the program stay with the church and nearly half serve as church volunteers.

Eight Recovery Principles based on the BEATITUDES
by Rick Warren

1. Realize I'm not God; I admit that I am powerless to control my tendency to do the wrong thing and my life is unmanageable.

"Happy are those who know they are spiritually poor." Matthew 5:3

2. Earnestly believe that God exists, that I matter to Him, and that He has the power to help me recover.

"Happy are those who mourn, for they shall be comforted." Matthew 5:4

3. Consciously choose to commit all my life and will to Christ's care and control.

"Happy are the meek." Matthew 5:5

4. Openly examine and confess my faults to God, to myself and to another person whom I trust.

"Happy are the pure in heart." Matthew 5:8

5. Voluntarily submit to any and all changes God wants to make in my life.

"Happy are those whose greatest desire is to do what God requires." Matthew 5:6

6. Evaluate all my relationships, offer forgiveness to those who have hurt me and make amends for harm I've done to others when possible, except when doing so would harm them or others.

"Happy are the merciful" Matthew 5:7 "Happy are the peacemakers" Matthew 5:9

7. Reserve a daily time with God for self-examination, Bible reading, and prayer in order to know God and His work for my life and gain the power to follow His will.

8. Yield myself to be used by God to bring this good news to others, both by my example and by my words.

"Happy are those who are persecuted because they do what God requires." Matthew 5:10

For more information or to find a Celebrate Recovery in your area, visit http://www.celebraterecovery.com.au/